The Loan Officer's Little Black Book

Copyright © 2009
All righs reserved

P.S. Publishing
ISBN 978-1-105-01264-8

Phil Leary

FORWARD

In the medical field, doctors keep on hand a convenient guide to aid them in certain aspects of their practice. The guide that they use is a staple in their profession; an indispensible tool called "THE PHYSICIAN'S DESK REFERENCE" (abbreviated as [a] "P.D.R.").

The Loan Officer's Little Black Book is designed to provide the same ready support for Loan Officers that a P.D.R. provides for medical doctors. The fusion of technical information and practical instruction makes this tool a unique and valuable resource - to be consulted time and again to inform or remind the proactive Loan Officer in both the sub-prime and prime sectors, of the varied aspects of their profession.

With knowledge comes ability, and with ability comes skill; with skill comes expertise, and with expertise comes respect; with respect comes trust, and with trust comes business, and with business comes profit - and therein lies the value of this book.

A loan officer can check out a book or a website for a glossary of mortgage terms. They may go to another website or check another book for essential mortgage calculations and formulas. They may resort to yet another site or book to find information related to credit or the appraisal, or purchase money, loan program distinctions, certain numeric code explanations, the financing and refinancing sequence of events, etc., but to find all of that - and more - in a single tangible reference is hard to come across. *This is such a reference*: a kind of one-stop-shop for L.O.'s. While websites can be wonderful resources, computers crash and power fails but books never fail - and good books never go out of style.

Designed for real-time application in a real-world scenario, the material in this reference focuses on the most common and immediate aspects of mortgage lending.

This book is not intended to be an end-all resource, but rather a hard-hitting, quick and easy reference, tailored for practical use for both the new Loan Originator and the experienced Loan Officer; presented in a friendly blend of shoptalk and technical jargon.

DEDICATIONS:

This book is kindly dedicated to:

Lennette Allen
Sue Babcock
Ralph Blanks
Michael Clark
Ann Lorring (Clark)
Carla Davis
Sam Ellison
Martin Holguin
Fabiola Hunter
Mr. David Jacobs
Olivia Jiminez
Ms Lie
Melissa Moss
Akbar Nabaa
Nick Njavaro
Angela Provo
Preet Saran
Justin Adam Willis
Betsy Zugzda

Jerry Torres & Yolanda Cordova

This books is also dedicated to the many other Loan Officers unnamed (though not forgotten) whom I had the pleasure and profit of working with, who allowed me to grow by sharing what I learned with them and whom I learned from again. I also owe a debt of gratitude to the all of the Processors, Appraisers, Account Executives, Title rep's, Underwriters and such who helped get me up to speed. Thank you all. In addition to my personal acquaintances, this book had in mind the many L.O.'s from "newbies" to the oldies-but-goodies, who seek to continually grow and to broaden their knowledge base; to hone the skills of their vocation and sharpen the pencil of their execution.

Becoming a bona fide L.O. can be tough and the learning curve can be long. I remember struggling as a new L.O., being provided little to no training, frustrated, broke and feeling overwhelmed, with no ready resources to remedy my confusion. I am thankful that there were Loan Officers within reach who were willing to help me as best they could when they could but I could not retain all that they told me in passing; needless to say, it wasn't working for me; nevertheless, I was bound and determined to learn my job and decided that when I did learn the ropes, I would commit what I learned to writing for my immediate recollection and benefit, and for the benefit of others by extension. I would spend four consecutive years (2002-2006) documenting my job while doing my job; all the while, checking and crosschecking, cross-referencing and confirming the things I learned in the larger arena of mortgage lending. And thus is the story of the creation of this material.

I readily acknowledge that I do not know everything there is to know about mortgage lending (I don't anyone who does), nor can I anticipate the changes that will take place in the marketplace in the future but I have been privileged to learn a great deal and wish to celebrate the scope of that knowledge by sharing it with others who have a passion to excel, and excellence comes with mastering "the nuts and bolts" of the job, which is what this reference provides -- and then some.

Upon training numerous Loan Officers with this same material, its real worth was tested and manifested in the reactions and comments of the Loan Officers themselves, saying as follows (*all quotes used by permission*):

"This is really great…wow…there's so much in here"
– Lennette Allen, Sr. Processor

"It's all in there - everything you need to know your job!"
– Sue Babcock, Sr. Loan Officer

*"Coming from a catering background, your training manual gave
me the opportunity to get a head start in the loan business."*
– Ralph Blanks, Independent Loan Consultant

*"The best piece of wood that hands have ever touched; the wood of
the pencil that wrote this book: my friend indeed, Mr. Phil Leary"*
– Ann Lorring (Clark), L.O./Processor

"Phil's book was a God-send"
– Michael Clark, Loan Consultant

*"I went to a library and checked out a book about mortgages, and
your book had more knowledge and more stuff…"*
– Carla Davis, Loan Officer

*"This reference should be on the desktop of every Loan Officer…
Knowing this information is the difference between being an LO
and a PRO. This little book is powerful!
Indeed good things come in small packages, as they say"*
– Sam Ellison, Independent Loan Consultant

*"If every new Loan Officer had this book, their job would be a
lot easier to understand because everything they need to know
is in there."*
– Ms Lie, certified Loan Originator & Processor

"If I'd had this information, I would have done better on my real estate exam because there are questions on the test that are covered in this book."
– Fabiola Hunter, Independent Loan Consultant

"That book has been a tremendous help to me. I read it all time I even read it in the bathroom!"
– Mr. David Jacobs, Loan Officer

"Your book Phil was easy to read - and easy to understand. It helped me a lot."
– Olivia Jiminez, Independent Loan Consultant

"This is like The Loan Officer's Bible!"
– Melissa Moss, Loan Officer

"This is the stuff they should be telling you"
– Angela Provo, Independent Loan Consultant

"I find Phil Leary's book not only to be educational and informational, but also a great quick reference guide for any loan officer wanting an edge in this competitive industry. Loan Officers can read it and refer back to it often; lenders and brokers can train new loan officers with it, and veterans can brush up with its easy-to-read format."
– Preet Saran, Independent Loan Consultant

"Oh, I still use that book. That book has helped me so much"
– Betsy Zugzda, Sr. Loan Officer

TABLE OF CONTENTS

DISCLAIMER:

While the information contained in this book was current and correct at the time of creation, the market is subject to fluctuation; accordingly, certain aspects of certain procedures may have undergone market-change - with the change in the economy; nevertheless, it will prove easy enough for an L.O. to make necessary adjustments in real time to conform to prevailing rules. Moreover, it doesn't hurt and even helps to have an understanding of some of the history and development or progression of industry *modus operandi,* terminologies and "shoptalk". This reference is valuable in that regard as well. But for the most part - and fortunately - the mechanics or principles of mortgage lending merely suffer a change in complexion - not in fundamentals.

While the author is confident in the soundness of the material, the author cannot assume liability for damages incurred directly or indirectly as a result of error, omission or discrepancy that may have gone undetected. Again, the Loan Officer is encouraged to keep current with the market and verify the interpretation, application and execution of procedure, as required by their profession and regulation.

SECTION 1

TERMINOLOGY

The following terminologies and related definitions are applicable as expressed; however, there is a margin of variance, as term signification and qualification may change from time to time, and criteria from lender to lender may differ in one respect or another; nevertheless, the industry-standard information will prove helpful across the board.

ACCELERATED PAYMENT(S): By a homeowner making at least one additional mortgage payment within a year (all directed toward principal - and not exceeding a certain dollar amount in a month - as specified by the lender - or not exceeding the maximum percentage of the mortgage balance allowed by the lender: e.g. 20%, to avoid incurring a prepayment penalty), the loan term may be reduced by roughly five years. The borrower may do this more than once in a year, however, should they exceed the lender's maximum allowable "principal" reduction, a one-time prepayment penalty may be assessed. By making the additional mortgage payment(s) in a year, the borrower is able to achieve a shorter term without having to refinance to do so, and without being forced into the substantially higher payment that a structured shorter term would create. This effectively creates a type of term and payment option for the borrower; *viz.* they can maintain their low(er) thirty-year payment and still achieve a shorter term, depending on how disciplined and financially fortunate they may be. (This is the same principle that undergirds the BI-WEEKLY payment – explained below).

AMORTIZATION: The payment of a debt or obligation over a term of years. The amortization schedule for mortgages is based on a median 30-year term. The longer the term, the lower the payment, and the shorter the term, the higher the payment. A loan amortized at 30 or 40 years does not make it a 30 or 40-year "fixed" loan.

A.R.M.'s are amortized over 30 and 40 years but the fixed period is typically two to ten years in duration. Amortization only speaks of the *payment schedule* in terms of years - not the loan *type*.

- In a fully amortized loan, some 80% of the mortgage payment goes toward interest, and some 20% toward principal for about the first three years; afterward, the interest-to-principal ratio begins to adjust, applying more toward principle and less toward interest.

A.P.N. – Assessor Parcel Number: is assigned by the county Assessor to all privately owned parcels (plots of land) in a given County. The A.P.N. relates most immediately to the parcel upon which a structure sits but it also serves to identify the structure as well, without necessarily qualifying the structure's classification (e.g. manufactured vs. modular or personal vs. real estate). With the passage of Proposition 13 in 1978 for California, reassessment of real property by the Assessor is required as of the date of a change in ownership or completion of new construction. The increase in property assessment otherwise is limited to an inflation index not to exceed two percent (2%) per year, while the annual property tax burden is about one percent (1%) of a property's assessed value; however, the industry-standard property tax factor is 1.25%, which makes allowance for additional fees as provided by law.

APPRAISAL/APPRAISER: The determination of a property's value upon the inspection and professional assessment by a certified licensed appraiser, as per the standards of the Office of Real Estate Appraisers. (There are four levels of real estate appraiser qualification or licensing, they are: "AT": Appraiser Trainee License, "AL": Appraiser residential License, "AR": Appraiser certified Residential license, and "AG": Appraiser certified General License. The AG has the broadest qualification of all the levels and is particularly trained and licensed to conduct appraisals on properties of five or more units.

The AG is also qualified to appraise commercial property, high rises, storefronts, land, environmental, etc. The AR is the next level down from the AG and is licensed to conduct appraisals on 1-4 unit properties but not commercial-level properties. Lenders will accept appraisals from AG's and AR's but not AT's. AT's may prepare or produce appraisal reports for a certified licensed appraiser but they must be signed by the supervising AR or AG.

APPURTENANCE: Something subordinate to another more important thing: an accessory. That which belongs to something else: an adjunct, an appendage. Something annexed to another thing more worthy as principle and which passes as incident to it as a right of way or other easement (right of use over the property of another for a limited purpose, as right of passage) to land, e.g. an outhouse, barn, garden, orchard to a house.

A.P.R. - **A**nnual **P**ercentage **R**ate: The cost of credit expressed in terms of an annual rate. Although expressed in percentage form like an interest rate is, the annual percentage rate is *not* the *"interest rate"* paid monthly but is the *annualized* interest percentage of a loan as expressed by the actual rate of interest paid - *accounting for costs, i.e. fees and points.* The *monthly interest rate* applied to a loan is what the lender charges the borrower for the privilege of credit - irrespective of cost(s), and is determined by the borrower's credit profile and L.T.V., whereas the *A.P.R. is derived from the cost aspect of the loan, which includes the fees and points* or "costs" charged over and above the base loan amount. The A.P.R. is typically higher than the expressed or advertised Interest Rate on a loan, as it factors in the cost(s), which the monthly interest rate does not account for.

A.R.M. - **A**djustable **R**ate **M**ortgage. A mortgage where the term of years involves a limited fixed rate period, with the balance of the term becoming adjustable and subject to market conditions.

ARM's are typically set in 30 (and now 40) year long amortized combinations (more payment-friendly than 20 or 15 year terms). ARMs may be expressed as 2/28, 3/27, 5/25, 7/23, 10/20 by sub-prime lenders, and 3/1, 5/1, 7/1, 10/6 by prime lenders; expressed either way, the products are the same (10 year long fixed ARMs are also called "Hybrid" loans). The number on the left of the slash mark represents the fixed term, and the number on the right signifies the adjustable period. ARM'S are also called "SHORT-TERM" loans, as the fixed rate period is a short 2-10 year term. There is a typical 1%-3% maximum CAP or percentage increase during the first year that the loan becomes adjustable, and usually not more than a 1% increase at each adjustment thereafter, not to exceed a 6% maximum cap over the life of the loan.

ARM'S LENGTH: A loan transaction involving parties so closely related as to admit the inclination or concern of impropriety.

ARREARAGES: (That which is behind; comes after. Payment made after the payment was due). In distinction to rent payment, which is typically made some thirty days in advance, a mortgage payment is current to the date of payment; as such, the amount owed/paid thirty days later is technically in arrears (though not deemed delinquent).

A.R.V. (After Repair Value - for investors): The estimated value of a property after needed repairs have been performed on a "fix-and-flip" unit to fetch the highest **Fair Market Value.** As the terms imply, **ARV** is essentially the opposite of **"As Is"** [properties]. "As is" concerns what a vacated property may sell for in its raw condition without repairs or renovation; again, *as is* - as quickly as possible. The estimated ARV is used to gauge the expected profit from an expected sale after costs have been factored in and/or accounted for, such as the cost of acquisition, holding costs and other or "soft" costs.

BANK STATEMENTS: When calculating "income" from bank statements for wage earners, all deposits within the month are to be totaled (excluding transfers) and the sum divided by twelve to arrive at the monthly "income" figure.

- For resident-based self-employed persons or home-based workers, lenders may only accept 80% of deposits; and for self-employed persons renting an office, only 70% of deposits, in consideration of "overhead". Also, many lenders do not allow a combining of personal and business bank statements -- only one or the other.

BANKRUPTCY: Chapter 7 is a Personal bankruptcy filing for a complete discharge of credit-reporting debt. Chapter 11 is for Business "reorganization" to restructure the terms of debt(s) and *re*payment. Chapter 13 is also a Personal bankruptcy filing but with a [5-year] *re*payment schedule of outstanding (credit-reporting) debts. The different types of Bk's must meet specific qualifications with respect to financing or refinancing of real property, which may vary from lender to lender.

BASIS POINTS (also called "bips"): A basis point is 1/100 (one one-hundredth) of a (an interest rate) point. 25 basis points is 25% (.25) or ¼ of an interest rate point. Fifty "bips" equals one-half (.50) of one percentage point.

- "Rate adjustments" are measured in basis points. Example: for a borrower to obtain the Interest Only option, their starting rate would typically be "adjusted" upward of 25 basis points for privilege. Another example could be a borrower refinancing a non-owner occupied property, for which, there might be a ¾ or .75 basis point increase or "hit" to the rate. (Not all adjustments increase the rate. Certain adjustments may decrease the rate. Each lender has their own set of criteria and guidelines).

BENEFIT-TO-BORROWER ("B-TO-B"):   In reaction to "predatory" lending, a control was implemented in mortgage lending referred to as "Benefit-To-Borrower". This rule was designed to ensure that there is a meaningful and tangible benefit to the borrower to justify the loan, and there are qualifying criteria to "test" the benefit question. Though criteria, limits and strictness may vary among lenders, following are the four loan aspects that lenders scrutinize for "B-TO-B". At least one of the four aspects must qualify.

1. LOAN TYPE: Converting an ARM to a Fixed loan program usually qualifies as B-TO-B.

2. SAVINGS: The borrower's monthly savings must, over a 60-month (five year) period, recoup the non-recurring closing costs of the loan (e.g. the appraisal fee, doc' drawing fee, escrow and title fees, notary fee, odd-days interest, processing, origination and rebate points, wire transfer fee, etc.), to satisfy B-TO-B.

3. CASH-OUT: The cash due to the borrower (which includes the amount for debt consolidation) must be at least 200% (or two times) the sum total of the non-recurring costs of the loan and the prepayment penalty (when applicable) to meet B-TO-B.

4. SEASONING: There usually needs to be 12 months ("seasoning") between refinance transactions for the lender to consider it beneficial rather than detrimental to the borrower. The rational behind this rule is that homeowners refinancing repeatedly and rapidly may be doing so as a way to subsidize their mortgage payment, which may be beyond their normal income means to pay; if so, doing so may be putting them further behind and deeper in the hole on their mortgage.

BI-WEEKLY PAYMENT: Taking the minimum monthly mortgage payment and dividing it by two (such amount to be paid every two weeks) creates twenty-six half-payments in a year instead of 12 single/whole payments. Paying every two weeks - totaling 26 payments in a year - covers all 52 weeks in the year equally; whereas, paying once a month and making what would be equal to only 24 half-payments in a year falls short of capitalizing on all 52 weeks (as there are months in a year with more than four weeks). The 26 half payments results in one extra mortgage payment per year - without any increase to the mortgage payment - which has the effect of lessening the loan term by roughly five years when done.

BONDS: A bond is a debt "security" (i.e. assurance of [re]payment or performance -- a type of I.O.U.). When a person purchases a bond, they are in effect lending money to the issuing entity (e.g. a government, federal agency, municipality, Corporation, or other "issuer"); and for the loan (the purchased bond), the issuer promises to pay back the obligation at a specified rate of interest for the duration of the bond, and to repay the face value or principal amount when it comes due, or "matures". The U.S. Treasury issues three types or levels of securities: 1) "BILLS", which have a maturity of less than one year. 2) "NOTES", which have a maturity of two to ten years. 3) "BONDS", which have a maturity of greater than ten years. U.S. Treasury securities are considered to have the lowest risk and to be the safest of all investments in the bond market because they are guaranteed by the "full faith and credit" of the united states government (i.e. the government's power of taxation and authority to print currency); as such, they are viewed as having no credit risk, owing to the certainty of the government's ability to pay back the loan. As a result, the interest rates on U.S. Treasury securities are generally lower than the rates on other widely traded debt, such as corporate bonds.

BRIDGE LOAN (also called "interim financing", "gap financing" or "swing-loan"):

Based on equity, this *interim* stage of financing may be sought when someone, who currently owns a property, wants to buy another property but have not been able to sell their current property, and need money to lay claim to the other property they wish to buy (at which time they will acquire "permanent" financing). In a typical bridge loan scenario, it is structured to pay off the balance of the existing mortgage, and the money remaining (minus closing costs and six months prepaid interest) can be used as a down payment toward the other property. When the currently owned property is sold, the bridge loan is paid off. The bridge loan is a short-term loan (up to one year). If the property does not sell within six months, the borrower must begin paying on the loan. Bridge loans come with high interest rates, points and other fees.

Bridge loans can be acquired by individuals or corporations and therefore may be structured a number of different ways. Essentially, a bridge loan is sought to fill the time "gap" where capital is needed to meet a present need to accomplish a future objective. It fills the space between point A and point B where funds may be inadequate.

BUY-DOWN: When the Loan Officer or Borrower buys the interest rate down - by paying the lender to do so. For fuller explanation, see "Discount Point" below and "Discount/Buy-down Points" in the "Basic Mortgage Calculations" of Section 6.

BUY-UP: An increase in the interest rate to buy, achieve or compensate for an exception for some aspect of the loan, e.g. LTV, credit score, prepayment penalty buy-out, rebate.

CAPITAL GAINS TAX/CGT (cf. 1031-Exchange in Section 2):

CAPITAL: "Accumulated goods, possessions, and assets used for the production of profits and wealth; an owners' equity in a business. Often used equally correctly to mean the total assets of a business. Sometimes used to mean capital assets."

GAIN: "Profits, winnings; increment of value; the difference between receipts and expenditures; pecuniary gain; the difference between cost and sale price. Appreciation in value or worth of securities or property" "excess of revenues over expenses from a specific transaction." "Gain derived from capital" is a gain, profit, or something of exchangeable value proceeding from the property, severed from the capital however invested, and received or drawn by claimant for his separate use, benefit and disposal.

ASSETS: "Property of all kinds, real and personal, tangible and intangible including *inter alia*, patents and causes of action which belong to any person, including a corporation and the estate of a decedent. The entire property of a person, association, corporation or estate that is applicable or subject to the payment of his or her or its debts."

CAPITAL GAIN(S): An increase in the value of a capital asset, investment or real estate that gives it a higher worth or "gain" over the purchase price. The profit realized on the sale or exchange of a capital asset.

- Essentially, the gain is the difference between the cost and the net proceeds from the sale or exchange of a capital asset. A [capital] "gain" is realized when a property is sold for more than is owed on the loan, and taxation is only assessed on the difference or "gain" from such a transaction. The gain is not realized until the asset is liquidated or sold for a profit. If by the time such an asset is sold or given away there has been an increase in value, the "gain" or "profit" portion of the sale or gift may be taxable.

However, the tax normally does not apply to the sale of personal belongings worth $10,000 U.S. dollars or less; or cars, lottery winnings, premium bonds, gilt (involving gold), certain other gains, and what qualifies as one's principal private residence/home (as opposed to investment property – considered a "capital asset"). Such are typically exempt from the capital gains tax.

- A capital gain may be short-term (one year or less) or long-term (more than one year), and must be claimed on one's income taxes. Formerly in the income tax laws, the profits from the sale of capital assets were taxed at separate and lower rates than applied to ordinary income; however, since the Tax Reform Act of 1986, long term capital gains are treated and taxed as ordinary income. Assets held for investment, such as stocks, bonds and real estate are considered "capital assets", whereas depreciable property, inventory and supplies that are costs of goods sold, are not. A Federal tax is imposed on gains from the sale of appreciable property. If a property is a "capital" asset, then the gain or loss is a "capital" gain or loss.

- Prior to the Tax Relief Act of May 7, 1997, the only way a homeowner could avoid paying taxes on a home-sale profit/gain was to apply the profit to the purchase of another, more-expensive house within two years. However, the Taxpayer Relief Act of 1997, provided for home-sale exemption(s), where homeowners do not have to purchase another house with the proceeds from the sale of their principal residence to avoid taxation. Furthermore, there is no limit to the number of times a homeowner can use the home-sale exemption (however, the law dictates that a homeowner must own and occupy the property they intend to sell for two out of five years to be eligible for the exemption).

Unlike before, homeowners can now enjoy discretionary use of tax-free profits of up to $250,000 or $500,000 depending on filing status (single or married) each time they sell their primary residence. This is a quantum improvement from the limited 'roll-over' rule of prior years, which did not allow homeowners to enjoy the proceeds from the sale of their principal residence - that is, without "capital gains" taxation - it only allowed them to avoid taxation of the proceeds; and the $125,000 maximum tax-exemption from the proceeds of a home-sale that was available to homeowners aged 55 and older was a once-in-a-lifetime occurrence.

CARRY BACK (re: purchases):   When a seller reduces the down payment burden of the buyer by creating/documenting a "private" second lien against the property, executed between the seller and the buyer alone, outlining the terms as agreed upon in the amount that the down payment will be reduced by or "carried back". The contract is to be signed, attested by both parties and recorded, making it binding. If the buyer breaches the contract, the seller may reclaim the property, having due recourse at law.

CLA: Conditional Loan Approval form: The document from the lender that shows the approval terms and pending conditions that must be satisfied in order for the loan documents to be drawn for the borrower's signature (called PTD - Prior To Doc's conditions.   Conditions to be met Prior To Funding may be abbreviated PTF).

CLTV: Combined Loan To Value. Where the LTV of two or more liens (mortgage loans) are combined to arrive at the total Loan To Value.

C.O.E.: Close Of Escrow

COLLECTIONS: Ironically, paying collection accounts off may initially negatively impact the credit score. The reason this may happen is because when collections (particularly aged collections) are brought current, they are in a sense 'renewed' and re-viewed as open accounts, which may appreciably increase the debt load and at the same time uncover gross delinquencies, both of which can individually work to suppress the credit score. The older collections become, the less they tend to matter, but bringing them current/paying them off is like opening an old wound, that, in a real sense, make take a month or two to heal.

COMBINATION LOAN: Typically (expressed as) an 80/20, meaning that a loan of 100 % LTV is broken up into two parts: the first lien/loan at 80% and the second at 20%. There are various other combinations of <100% C.L.T.V. but the 80%/20% combo is the most common. In a combination loan, a first position lien at 80% or less is desirable as such tends to avoid P.M.I., whereas combos with the first position lien starting above 80% is likely to encounter P.M.I. Also, for loans of 100% LTV, the 80%/20% combo loan has universal acceptance and application, whereas the "100%-straight" loan is a sub-prime or VA specialty product (not offered by prime lenders as a rule).

COMMERCIAL REAL ESTATE PROPERTY: Property designed, intended and zoned for "commercial" (business) use. A classification of real estate that includes income-producing property such as office buildings, gasoline stations, restaurants, shopping centers, hotels and motels, parking lots and stores; in other words, property used for public accommodation(s). Apartment complexes or structures with more than four units are also deemed commercial property. The "commercial" category falls between the residential and industrial categories of real estate.

COMP'S (short for "comparables"):

The value of neighboring properties, "compared" to the subject property, are used to determine the probable value of the subject property. When viewing comp's on paper, the key characteristics to identify are the year built and the square footage of the structure. (The lot size does not appreciably impact the comparison between properties unless there is a 10,000 or more square foot difference between the parcels). The properties closest in date range and square footage to the subject property would be the most "comparable". A subject property's probable value is established by the three most comparable properties in the area (on average, limited to a one mile radius).

COMPENSATING FACTORS: Enhancing or mitigating aspects about a borrower's circumstances that may incline the lender to make an exception for their qualification. For example, a borrower may seek or need an LTV exception where their credit may not qualify to achieve what they want. A "compensating factor" of the borrower's profile could be that they have been employed in their occupation and/or with their current employer for over 10 consecutive years. Another compensating factor could be that they have had an unblemished payment history over the last 2 years. Such enhancing or mitigating aspects about the borrower could persuade a lender to grant the exception requested.

COMPRESSION: When buying down the interest rate by more than one point, the cost-to-buy-down ratio begins to drop or "compress"; e.g., whereas the first buy-down point may reduce the interest rate by 50 "bips", the second buy-down point may only reduce the rate by 30 or 40 more "basis points", and so on. Lenders typically have a two-point buy-down maximum and each lender has their own buy-down rules, though the rules are fairly generic.

CONFORMING LOAN: An "A-paper" or "Prime" credit profile.

(i.e. where the middle of three or the lower of two credit scores is 680 or higher), as opposed to a "Sub-prime" credit profile (i.e. where the borrower's credit score is below 620). Conforming loans are also called "Freddie Mac" or "Fannie Mae" loans (i.e. loans structured to conform to the standards for sale on the secondary market to FHLMC ("Freddie Mac") or FNMA ("Fannie Mae"). There is also such a thing as a "conforming" loan amount (see "Jumbo" below).

CONSIDERATION: An inducement from one party to contract with another. An act or a promise to act offered by one party to persuade another to enter into a contract to act or to refrain from acting; something of value given in exchange for a promise. A consideration is distinguished from gift in that a gift is: "A voluntary transfer of property to another made gratuitously and without consideration", whereas consideration is a matter of quid pro quo. Even the mere promise to pay money is sufficient for "consideration", as such may induce another party to contract, and is based on the principle of reciprocation - rather than gratuity. Thus, in the case of purchasing property, an earnest money deposit is not necessary for purposes of creating a binding contract.

CONVENTIONAL LOAN: A mortgage or deed of trust that is not obtained under a government insured program, such as F.H.A. or V.A.

CONVEYANCE: The transferring of a property title from one individual to another. The instrument transferring title of land for one person - or group of persons - to an other(s). RECONVEYANCE: The transferring of a title back to its previous owner. A (deed of full) reconveyance removes the lien that a lender placed against a property when a loan on the property was originally acquired, and a title search will show that the lien (and note) has been paid in full or satisfied.

COST: An aspect of the loan that "costs", meaning that the borrower or the Loan Officer will be charged for a benefit unattainable without the extra cost (e.g. a discount point or Prepayment Penalty buyout).

COST CALCULATION: Multiply the total loan amount by the cost factor percentage and add that figure to the previous total loan amount for the new loan amount (see example in section 6 Basic Mortgage Calculations below).

CREDIT SCORE or "FICO" (standing for: Fair Isaac COmpany): Credit rating or numeric score, roughly and conventionally 350 - 850 (and since 2006, 501 - 990 by "VantageScore": a credit reporting system utilized by all three credit repositories - Experian, Equifax and Beacon - to compete with "FICO"), determined by a number of credit related factors, such as credit payment history, derogatory history (e.g. bankruptcy, Notice Of Default, Foreclosure, etc. Also see CREDIT RISK FACTORS below). Following are six tiers of credit ranges, which may vary from lender to lender: from sub-prime to prime.

680-850 = "A-paper" / "Prime" credit.
679-620 = "Alt-A paper" (between "Prime" and "sub-prime").
619-580 = "B-paper" (sub-prime)
579-550 = "C-paper" (sub-prime)
549-500 = "D-paper" (sub-prime)
499-400 = "E-paper" (sub-sub-prime)

The credit score is subject to drop when a borrower experiences late payments, BK's, NOD, foreclosure, collections/charge-off's, heavy debt load and multiple "inquiries". Theoretically (which may differ from practice), any number of inquiries made within a 14-day period related only to mortgage or auto is treated as a single inquiry, and all inquiries made 30 days prior to a new inquiry are supposedly ignored; however, inquiries made by other institutions outside of mortgage and auto (regardless of the time period) counts as a separate and additional inquiry each time the credit is run.

This may cause a reduction in the credit score (by 1 point per repository, per inquiry, if not more). Although "Fico score" is the most commonly used term in referring to consumer's credit score(s), there are actually three major credit repositories that report consumer credit scores (but all based on the **Fair Isaac Company**/FICO model). They are:

- BEACON, a.k.a. "EQUIFAX"/EFX (dominates the southern section of the U.S.)

- FAIR ISAAC, a.k.a. "EXPERIAN"/XPN (CA-based: dominates the west coast)

- TRANS UNION, a.k.a. "EMPERICA"/TU (dominates the east coast)

A credit report that features the scores from all three credit repositories is called a "tri-merge" or "3-bureau in-file" report. Mortgage lenders typically require all three bureaus' scores, and use the middle of the three scores or the lower of two as the qualifying score. (There are exceptional cases where certain lenders may take an average of all three scores or use a "single-bureau score" or the highest credit score - for pricing purposes only, not for qualification. Research groups have determined that upwards of 95% of credit reports have upwards of 25% error, underscoring the importance of knowing one's credit profile.

DEBT CONSOLIDATION: Consolidating consumer debt - particularly high interest bearing credit card liabilities in a low-interest mortgage refinance yields two special benefits: 1) A substantial reduction in the interest rate(s) on the outstanding balance(s), resulting in considerable savings. 2) Tax deductibility. Consumer/credit card debt is not tax deductible but residential mortgage [interest] is. The credit card loan balances do not disappear when they are "paid off" through a mortgage refinance, rather, they are transferred to the new mortgage balance.

Nevertheless, the borrower's overall monthly outgo may be substantially reduced by the newly structured lower interest rate on the overall debt(s).

DEBT-TO-INCOME-RATIO: The ratio of outgo-to "in-come" (expressed in percentage form). With prime lenders, the maximum debt ratio (as structured in a new purchase or refinance transaction) is typically 35%-40%. With Alt-A lenders: 40%-45%, and with sub-prime lenders: 50% on "stated" deals and 55% full doc' deals. The reason that sub-prime lenders draw the line at 50%-55% is because experience has shown that borrowers with debt ratios above that level are prone to [first] payment default. Depending on the program, the debt ratio may be divided into two parts: "Top" and "Bottom":

- "Top" relates to the "Payment-To-Income" Ratio, which is calculated by dividing the total monthly mortgage payment (PITI - of the primary residence/subject property) by the total gross monthly "income". The "Top" or Payment-To-Income Ratio differs from the "Bottom" or "Debt-To-Income ratio" in that it only accounts for the mortgage debt, not the borrower's total debt, thus it is not a complete or true picture or ratio of "income"-to-outgo, which is what the "Bottom" or the Debt-To-Income Ratio speaks to.

- "Bottom" relates more precisely to the idea of "Debt-To-"Income" ratio (as opposed to "payment-to-income ratio") as it is calculated by dividing the total monthly debt payments ("outgo") by the total gross monthly "income".

Another (more common) way of looking at D.T.I.R. is: Front-end vs. Back-end:

- "Front-end" debt ratio (differing from "Top" or P.T.I.) is the total of all credit-reporting debt excluding a mortgage payment divided by the borrower's "income" (applicable to financing property).

- "Back-end" debt ratio (like "Bottom" ratio) is the total of all credit-reporting debt, including the mortgage payment divided by the borrower's "income" (applicable to refinancing property).

DEED: A conveyancing (transferring) or financing instrument (document) given to pass fee (ownership) title to property upon sale.

DEED-IN-LIEU: A deed in lieu *of foreclosure* is a legal instrument (in writing; a document) whereby the borrower (the "mortgagor") surrenders (or "conveys") all interest in the subject real property to the lender (or "mortgagee") to satisfy the loan when in default in an effort to avoid foreclosure.

DEED OF TRUST (also called a "T.D." for "Trust Deed"): An instrument/document often used in place of a mortgage. Property is transferred by the trustor (borrower) to a trustee in favor of the lender (beneficiary) and is reconveyed/returned (to the trustor) upon payment in full. In other words, the true and acknowledged owner of a property is the lender until such time the borrower finishes paying it off, which is held in trust, evinced by the "Deed of Trust" until payment is satisfied, and during which time, the trustee has a fiduciary obligation to the lender, not the borrower. A trust deed is similar to a mortgage - the main difference is that a deed of trust involves three parties: the mortgagor, the trustee and the mortgagee, whereas a mortgage involves only two parties: the mortgagor (borrower/debtor) and the mortgagee (lender).

DELEGATED: A "delegated" loan is one that is *underwritten* by the lender directly. A non-delegated loan is one that is not underwritten directly by the [Direct] lender but by the purchasing Wholesale lender.

DEROG'S: Derogatory marks reflected on a credit and/or title report (e.g. Bankruptcy, N.O.D., foreclosure, late payments).

DISCHARGED VS. DISMISSED:

DISCHARGE: "To...dismiss. To extinguish an obligation (e.g. a person's liability on an instrument)." (Black's Law Dic.). The discharge of a debt (e.g. bankruptcy) is a voluntary and lawful release of a debtor from his debts, and being lawful, acceptable; as such, lenders are inclined to show leniency for discharges.

DISMISSAL: "To discontinue. An order or judgment finally disposing of an action, suit, motion, etc., without trial of the issues involved. Such may be voluntary or involuntary" (Black's Law Dic.).

As concerns bankruptcy (e.g. chapter 13), a dismissal is an involuntary interruption and unsatisfactory termination of a debtor's repayment arrangement (as scheduled by law) to his creditors for failure to keep or satisfy the terms of the schedule; and being unsatisfactory, unacceptable; as such, lenders are less lenient with dismissals than they are with discharges.

DISCOUNT POINT: Discounting or buying down the rate can be accomplished one of several ways: 1) Cost of the buy-down/discount point(s) can be charged to the borrower by adding what the discount point(s) translates into dollar-wise to the overall loan amount. 2) The L.O. may opt to commute commission point(s) to a discount/buy-down purpose of a loan. 3) L.O. may introduce the interest rate one point above the qualifying rate, to make allowance for the probability of needing to buy the rate down, when a borrower's credit or qualification appears uncertain (accomplishing the first option proactively).

DISPOSABLE "INCOME": The part of one's earnings or "income" that remains after taxes have been deducted.

It is called "disposable" because what is left after taxes is free to be disposed of at the discretion of the individual. (The individual has no "discretion" over the taxable portion of their earnings; that is "disposed of" by the government). One's disposable earnings is also loosely referred to as "spendable income", as it represents the monies left to spend or save as the individual wishes, yet differing from:

"DISCRETIONARY INCOME": What is left of one's "disposable" earnings after "fixed" obligations and necessities have been satisfied (e.g. mortgage/rent, car payment(s), credit cards, insurance(s), utilities, food, etc.); differing yet from "NET INCOME", defined as: the "income subject to taxation after allowable deductions and exemptions have been subtracted from gross income". The order of decreasing dominance of the three types of "income" discussed above may be viewed as: NET, then DISPOSABLE, then DISCRETIONARY.

D.U. / A.U. - Desktop Underwriting / Automatic Underwriting: Underwriting done through an automated system or pricing engine that readily provides approval or disapproval ratings and Conditional Loan Approval stipulations, in distinction to traditional manual underwriting, a process which may take several days to complete when done by an individual. (The acronym DU may also be used for "Delegated" Underwriting: underwriting performed by the ["Direct"] lender directly, rather than a Wholesale/Broker "lender").

EARLY PAYOFF PENALTY: When the lender demands repayment of the YSP from the broker for a loan that was paid off early (via refinance, sale or by other means). The broker in turn is likely to extract the monies from the loan officer who sold the loan. The early payoff penalty differs from the prepayment penalty in that the Prepayment Penalty affects or penalizes the borrower, whereas the Early Payoff Penalty penalizes the broker who may penalize the loan officer.

ENCUMBRANCE: A lien or liability attached to and binding real property.

EQUITY: The difference between the (appraised) property value and the total mortgage balance(s). Put another way: The market value of real property minus the amount of existing liens.

ESCROW: A neutral and unbiased agency or holding company (a third party) that a buyer and seller (borrower and lender) use to conduct a transaction.

"FARMER MAC" (FAMC): The Federal Agricultural Mortgage Corporation: Serves as a secondary market in agricultural loans such as mortgages for agricultural real estate and rural housing.

FEE SIMPLE: i.e., OWNERSHIP - in which the owner of the estate is entitled to unrestricted powers to dispose of the property as they wish, and which can be left by will or inheritance.

"FREDDIE MAC" (FHLMC) - Federal Home Loan Mortgage Corporation: A federal agency purchasing conventional and federally insured mortgage loans (on the secondary market) from members of the Federal Reserve System and the Federal Home Loan Bank.

FINANCE CHARGE: The cost of credit expressed in dollars.

"FANNIE MAE" (FNMA): Federal National Mortgage Association (a private corporation -- monitored by the Fed's) dealing in the purchase of mortgage loans on the secondary market at discounts.

(Freddie Mac & Fannie Mae grew out of the conforming/prime market's unwillingness to provide alternative products to embrace the sub-prime sector which the Fed's wanted to introduce for the purpose of stimulating the housing market. As such, the conforming/prime market and the non-conforming/sub-prime market are based on different standards; one of the salient differences is the extent of disclosure. The sub-prime market must provide a HUD and other documentation fully disclosing the charges related to a loan; the prime market also provides disclosure but does not have to, to the extent that the sub-prime sector has to. As it turned out, the sub-prime market had become so lucrative that the prime market came to embrace and support it with products and services of their own).

F.H.A. The Federal Housing Administration grew out of the National Housing Act of 1934, which was created for the purpose of stimulating the housing market, which in turn would stimulate the economy (that was gripped by the great depression) by providing for the jobs necessary to accomplish the task of building a market of affordable housing for low to moderate "income" people, who otherwise could not have afforded or qualified to own a house. The idea was to start the program with government subsidy but with a goal to have it become self-supporting by the insurance premiums that would be required of the borrowers.

- In 1965 the FHA became part of the Department of Housing and Urban Development or "HUD"; thereafter, referred to as the FHA & HUD. (The FHA is the only government agency that is completely self-funded, operating solely from its own income, and at no cost to taxpayers).

- The FHA does not lend money to borrowers but rather creates and manages the guidelines that federally approved lenders must practice. As a federal agency, the FHA insures the lender against loss of principle in the event that the borrower defaults on the loan.

- An FHA loan is a government-insured loan -- insured by the United States government.

- FHA loan limits fluctuate but the range is between the low to moderate price level. A standard FHA loan is not suitable for high-priced properties.

- An FHA loan can be advantageous for first-time homebuyers, as it offers the most relaxed and flexible guidelines for mortgage loans requiring < 5% down payment, such as:

  1. A ~~580~~ 620-660 credit score threshold

  2. Only 2 years employment history required (preferably with the same employer), with no "income" limits; however, lenders look for the most recent 2 years earnings to reflect a constant or increased amount.

  3. Bk's after 2 years old with a pursuant 2 consecutive years of good credit history.

  4. Foreclosures after 3 years old with a pursuant 3 consecutive years of good credit history.

  5. (The borrower's new mtg. payment should not exceed 30% of their gross monthly earnings).

- FHA loans do not have a Prepayment Penalty; however, a one time upfront kind of PMI, more accurately called: MMI, MIP or UFMIP (Mutual Mortgage Insurance, Mortgage Insurance Premium or Up Front Mortgage Insurance Premium) is factored into the loan, which can be paid out of pocket at closing or financed through the loan itself. Additionally, there is a monthly Mortgage Insurance ("MI") factored into the loan as well. Depending on the borrower's credit score, the MMI/MIP (or the one time "upfront" Mutual Mortgage Insurance Premium) range will be between 1.25% and 2.25% of the opening balance of the loan.

The MI (or monthly Mortgage Insurance) range will be 50% to 55% of the opening loan balance.

- The one-time, up front Mortgage Insurance Premium is usually financed into the loan and prorated over 5 years (meaning that if the buyer refinances or sells the property within the first 5 years, they may receive a partial refund of the UFMIP paid at the inception of the loan). As a rule, MI is paid for 5 years or until such time the loan balance is paid down to 78% of the appraised value; whichever occurs first. Also, MI may be negated if the borrower can provide a 10% down payment on a 15 year term or longer.

FIXED RATE: (Also referred to as "long-term" - in distinction to the "short-term" Adjustable Rate Mortgage loan products). An interest rate that remains stable or "fixed" throughout the term of the loan - again, as distinguished from an A.R.M., that becomes unstable after the brief fixed rate term of the loan matures).

FLOOR RATE: The absolute lowest interest rate the lender will offer the borrower (to protect and ensure the lender's profitability). This rate may also be expressed as the "start rate" on lenders' pricing matrices. (The floor rates on A.R.M. products are typically lower than the floor rates on fixed products).

FORECLOSURE: "A proceeding in equity [i.e., "Justice administered according to fairness as contrasted with the strictly formulated rules of common law...the object of which is to render the administration of justice more complete by affording relief where the courts of law are incompetent to give it..."], whereby a mortgagee either takes title to or forces the sale of the mortgagor's property in satisfaction of a debt. Procedure by which mortgaged property is sold on default of mortgagor in satisfaction of a mortgage debt...

If proceeds from the sale fail to pay debt in full, mortgagee creditor may obtain a Deficiency judgment" (Black's Law Dictionary, Sixth Edition). Foreclosure implements some 90 days after a Notice Of Default has been recorded against the delinquent homeowner/borrower, and the foreclosure process may take another 90 days to finalize. Different lending institutions have differing criteria related to foreclosure with respect to real estate loan qualification. For example, conventional lenders (e.g., "Fannie Mae" and "Freddie Mac"), all things being equal, may provide a real estate loan to a borrower with a foreclosure in their history that is at least 5 years old. F.H.A. (a government sponsored program) may provide a real estate loan to a borrower with a foreclosure in their history that is at least 3 years old. V.A. (also a government sponsored program) may provide a real estate loan to a borrower with a foreclosure in their history that is at least 2 years old.

FULLY AMORTIZED LOAN: Payment of a debt in equal periodic installments of principal *and* interest scheduled or amortized to be paid off at the end of a term of years. (Interest Only and Neg' Am' programs may be seen as 'partial amortization' as they are designed to pay down only part or a portion of the loan balance.

FULL DOC': A fully documented loan; documenting the source of a borrower's earnings or "income". Required documentation includes the most recent 30 days of Y-T-D pay stubs and the most recent two years' W-2's for "wage earners"; or 12 or 24-months of bank statements or the two most recent years' 1099's or tax returns - for self-employed persons. Also "award letters" (from the government or a municipality evincing the amount and fixed period of the recipient's "award" or guaranteed stipend) may be used - or required - for disabled or retired persons. A co-borrower's earnings may only be used if the co-borrower(s) will be on the loan, in a full doc' situation.

- "Additional income" from sources other than wage-earnings/pay stubs, 1099's and such, that is not verifiable or cannot be documented as being guaranteed or reliable does not contribute to the "income" qualification of the loan.

"GINNIE MAE" (GNMA): The Government National Mortgage Association (the only mortgage-backed security that enjoys the full faith and credit of the U.S. Government). The GNMA, like the FHLMC/"Freddie Mac" and the FNMA/"Fannie Mae" is a secondary-market lender, providing many retail lenders funds for lending purposes. Secondary-market lenders help the national mortgage market by providing qualification regulations and guidelines that help the general public, and by facilitating the availability mortgage products and the movement of money from state-to-state so that mortgages are not limited to certain areas.

GOOD FAITH ESTIMATE - "G.F.E." (also loosely called a "Jiffy"): An itemized estimate of the costs of a loan, offered in good faith as being reasonable, though not exact or perfectly accurate, and as such, subject to refinement.

GRADING: In addition to credit score recognition, lenders apply a credit GRADE (typically A-D) to borrowers. Such grades are based upon the presence or absence of derogatory history. The credit grade, along with the credit score, determines the borrower's risk level and interest rate qualification.

GRANT DEED: One of many types of deeds, used to transfer real property. Importantly, a grant deed warrants that the grantor actually owned the title in order to transfer it - which a quitclaim deed does not necessarily do, which rather transfers the interest in, or portion of the property that the grantor owned, if any.

GROSS UP: An increase, typically up to .0125% above the expressed social security amount, to allow or compensate for taxation of the same (equivalent to gross "income"). Grossing up may also apply to VA benefits but not pensions and retirement.

H.A.F.A.: Home Affordable Foreclosure Alternatives program. For homeowners who cannot afford their mortgage payment and need to transition to more affordable housing, HAFA provides 2 (two) options for transitioning out of the mortgage: 1) A short sale. 2) Deed-in-Lieu (DIL) of foreclosure.

- In a short sale, the mortgagee (lender) allows the mortgagor (borrower) to sell their house for an amount less than or that falls "short" of the amount of the remaining balance.

- In a Deed-in-Lieu, the bank (or mortgage company or lender) allows the borrower to relinquish the title and transfer ownership back to the bank.

[H]ELOC ([Home] Equity Line Of Credit): A second mortgage lien against one's property, (based on credit and equity), which the homeowner may borrow from, at their discretion. The loan amount established is fixed or closed-ended; however, usage is open-ended, like a revolving credit card account. The homeowner may draw as much or as little as they wish up to the set loan amount. The portion of the loan amount that sits unused remains available to the borrower (as with a credit card). The minimum payment requirement on the amount borrowed is typically interest only.

- Should a borrower with a H.E.L.O.C. refinance and wish to consolidate or "wrap" the first and second (HELOC) loans into a single new loan, lenders require that the entire HELOC amount be paid off through the new loan, whether the entire amount was enjoyed by the borrower or not.

Why? Because it is the entire HELOC amount that is recorded as the lien against the property (not the amount enjoyed or expected to be used, as such is subject to change).

Benefits:

- Mortgagor is afforded free advice from HUD-approved housing counselors and licensed real estate professionals.

- In distinction to conventional short sales, a HAFA short sale fully releases the borrower from their mortgage debt upon selling the property, i.e. the borrower will no longer be liable for the amount that falls short of the balance owed. The difference is simply waived by the servicer.

- The lender works with the borrower to arrive at an agreeable sale price.

- H.A.F.A. causes less of a negative impact on the borrower's credit [score] than foreclosure or conventional short sales can create.

- At closing, HAFA *may* provide $3,000 in relocation assistance.

HMDA: Home Mortgage Disclosure Act - a Federal statute, enacted by congress in 1975 - involves the government enforced and monitored reporting of "public" loan data on borrowers (such as ethnicity, race, gender) that impacts marketing practices and is designed to correct unfair and discriminatory treatment of consumers/borrowers.

HOEPA (Home Ownership & Equity Protection Act): HOEPA is essentially an anti-gouging law. HOEPA was designed to protect homeowners from predatory practices (inordinate charges) on the part of the lender.

The HOEPA was implemented in 1994 to amend the Truth In Lending Act (TILA), which is governed by SECTION 32 of Regulation Z as issued by the Board of Governors of the Federal Reserve System in relation to the Consumer Credit Protection Act as amended (15 UNITED STATES CODE). HOEPA is more commonly referred to as "Section 32" or the "high-cost" limit rule.

This cost-controlling regulation dictates that the total costs (i.e. fees + points) of a first-position lien/loan - before or at closing - cannot exceed whichever is the larger of $499.00 (as of 2004) or 8% of the total loan amount and/or that the A.P.R. cannot exceed - by more than ten percentage points - the rates on Treasury securities of comparable maturity. In conventional mortgage lending, the standard approach is to limit the costs of a loan <= $250,000.00 to 6% of the total loan amount, and 7.5% on loans exceeding $250,000.00. To simplify matters, lenders multiply the total loan amount by 5.99% to ascertain the maximum cost figure, so as to stay safely within the bounds of the regulation. (The loan "cost" includes escrow, title, processing, administrative, wire, doc' drawing, notary fees, front and back-end points, discount/buy-down, buy-up points, etcetera).

HUD (also referred to as "HUD 1"): The HUD 1 is a R.E.S.P.A. form and is the settlement statement that discloses the breakout or breakdown of all of the loan charges and adjustments or "closing costs", and how they are to be assumed or received by all parties in connection with the loan. (The HUD should be provided at least one day prior to signing to have all charges confirmed or corrected).

IMPOUNDS: A monthly mortgage payment including taxes and insurance in addition to Principal and Interest.

INDEMNIFY / INDEMNITY: Synonyms: Protection, compensation, reparation, exemption, exoneration.

To give or to be given protection - as by insurance - from liabilities or penalties incurred by one's actions. To provide for compensation against anticipated loss or damages sustained, expenses incurred. To give or be given security against future liability.

INDEX/INDEXES/INDICES: A short-term variable measure affecting the interest rate on an adjustable rate mortgage loan. The index may also be viewed as the cost of borrowing money. Common residential mortgage indices include the C.M.T., C.O.D.I., the 11th district C.O.F.I., C.O.S.I. L.I.B.O.R., M.T.A., U.S. Treasury Securities Indexes, etc. Certain indexes (like the C.M.T., L.I.B.O.R. and T-Bill) offer the flexibility of a one, three, six, or twelve-month variability option. Other indices (like the 11th district C.O.F.I. and the M.T.A.) have the "lagging" or "trailing" characteristic; meaning that while the rate changes in real-time, the effect on the monthly payment may be delayed for some time.

SPECIFIC INDEXES/INDICES:

11TH DISTRICT: The F.H.L.B. (The Federal Home Loan Bank) system consists of 12 Districts, each, having its own 'District Bank'. The 11th District FHLB is based in San Francisco but the district includes member savings and loan banking institutions from Arizona, California and Nevada.

CMT (Constant Maturity Treasury indexes): The CMT is used by the Federal Reserve Board and lenders as a basis to build and determine the interest rate on A.R.M. loans. These indexes may represent weekly or monthly average yields on U.S. Treasury securities - adjusted to constant maturities. The CMT indexes are volatile and move with the market; reflecting the state of the economy, they respond quickly to economic changes. The CMT indexes react more slowly than the CD index, but more quickly than the COFI or the MTA indexes.

1-Year CMT Index: Used on about half of the ARM'S with annual (once-a-year) rate adjustments, making it the most widely used of the indexes. It is also referred to as the 1-Year T-Bill (Treasury bill), the 1-Year Treasury Security (1 Yr. T-Sec), or the 1-Year Treasury Spot index.

3-Year CMT Index: (3/27) ARM'S tied to this index will adjust at the three-year mark. It is also referred to as the 3-Yr T-Sec., for 3-Year Treasury Security index.

5-Year CMT Index: (5/25) ARM'S tied to this index will adjust at the five-year mark. (The ARM'S adjustment period is usually the same as the security's constant maturity).

CODI (Certificate Of Deposit Index/Cost Of Deposit Index): A CODI index is the aggregate sum of the return that banks are paying to their depositors on 3-month CD's (which is typically a very low rate of return - currently 1.40%). Banks are not inclined to increase the rate of return - for obvious reasons - as a result, the CODI index remains one of the most stable. (The way banks calculate the CODI is by taking the daily average of their 3-month CD's, and add those daily values together for one month, which is divided by the number of days in the month to reach a monthly value, which is added to the previous 11 monthly values and divide by 12 to arrive at the CODI Index).

COFI - The 11th District Cost Of Funds Index was introduced in 1981, meaning the weighted average cost of all funds from the member savings and loan banking institutions of the 11th District. The funds include the savings, checking, money market, and short term CD accounts and advances by the FHLB District Bank, and other borrowed monies.

The percentages vary from time to time, but at present, an approximate 60% of funds come from Checking and Savings accounts, while an approximate 30% of funds comes from 6-month and 1-years C.D.'s, and still another approximate 10% comes from 2-5-year Cash Deposits.

The COFI is a slow moving index that represents a weighted average of the cost of funds of short and long-term accounts, amounting to approximately $350 billion in assets.

The COFI on average does not move very quickly, accordingly, interest rates tied to it do not fluctuate quickly. (A "weighted average" takes into account the proportional relevance of each component, rather than treating each component equally). The Cost of Funds Index loan is not market-dependent and does not move with other indexes. The Cost Of Funds Index amounts to the cost for banks to do business, and as such, stays low and moves very slowly. COFI is calculated at the end of every month for the previous month, causing it to lag behind the overall market, which benefits borrowers when rates are on an upswing, but not when the rates on a downswing.

COSI (Cost Of Savings Index): This index is similar in nature to the COFI index but it is peculiar to one particular lender. The Lender borrows the money received from its clients in the form of cash deposits, checking and savings accounts with which it creates an index (to which it adds a margin) which it uses for home mortgages. The interest rates in effect on these deposits are the basis for the COSI. The COSI is not based on actual interest paid on deposit accounts but rather on a weighted annualized rate of all interest rates in effect on deposit accounts as of the last day of each month.

LIBOR (London InterBank Offered Rate): A short-term (six and twelve month) index rate based on a European monetary index, as established by the activity between specific European banks - represented by the Bank of London. It is the rate offered by the London Interbank community for U.S. dollar deposits of a stated maturity. As with other indexes, the LIBOR is used as a base for setting rates of ARM products, offering aggressive initial rates - often lower than rates of other ARM'S - it has been competitive with other ARM indexes such as the 11th District C.O.F.I., the 6-Month Treasury bill, and the 6-Month **Certificate Of D**eposit **I**ndex. (A 12-month LIBOR is used often as well).

MTA: 12-Month Treasury Average index. This index is based on the average annual monthly yields of U.S. Treasury Securities, (T-Bill) adjusted to a constant maturity of one year, as made available by the Federal Reserve. The index is determined by adding together the monthly yields for the most recent 12 months, divided by 12. As an average, higher yields in some months are offset by lower yields in others (this averaging-out dynamic makes the M.T.A. a preferable index for the Neg' Am' product. See NEG' AM' below).

- Rate increases take longer to affect the 12-month MTA than other ARM indices, making it preferable to other indices. The MTA/Monthly Treasury Average (also known as the M.A.T./12-Month Moving Average Treasury Index) is a relatively new ARM index representing the 12-month average of the monthly average yields of U.S. Treasury securities adjusted to a constant maturity of one year. It is calculated by averaging the previous 12 monthly values of the 1-year CMT (Constant Maturity Treasury). As an annual average, the MTA/MAT is steadier than the 1-year CMT index.

- The MTA and CODI indexes tend to fluctuate more than the 11th District COFI although their patterns are very similar. However, the MTA and 11th District COFI-indexed ARM'S share in common the characteristic that they both have the potential for negative amortization. The MTA is the most widely used index for the Option ARM product.

T-BILL INDEXES: The Treasury Bill indexes move with the market and respond quickly to economic changes like the CMT indexes. T-Bill indexes have both weekly and monthly values. Monthly values are averages of the past month's weekly T-Bill rates. The monthly 6-Month Treasury bill index (6-MoT-Bill) is the most often used. ARM'S tied to the 6-Month T-Bill usually adjust once every six months.

INTEREST ONLY LOAN (I/O): Interest only loans are typically offered on ARM'S but not often on fixed products. As a rule, the **Interest Only** payment feature of the loan is good for five and even ten years (regardless of the fixed period of the A.R.M.), after which time the loan coverts to full amortization, however the principle balance of the loan will have interest factored into it (in other words, paying the interest (only) portion of the loan for five or ten years does not make the balance of the loan interest free). And there is usually a "rate adjustment" for the I/O option and a credit score requirement to qualify for it. (Lenders' credit criteria vary). Also:

- Taxes and Insurance must be factored into the loan payment as part of qualifying the borrower, whether or not the mortgage payment will be impounded.

- The principle balance may be reduced but not more than 20% of the loan amount per year without a penalty being incurred. The portion of the principle that is reduced will not have interest applied to it.

- On average, the I/O payment is $150.00 - $200.00 lower than a fully amortized payment.

- The I/O loan is strategic for investors and attractive to first-time homebuyers for various reasons.

- As Interest Only loans involve the payment of interest only, it may be viewed as only a "partially amortized" loan, as opposed to a fully amortized loan, which involves the simultaneous payment of principle and interest.

INTEREST RATE: The Interest rates on short-term and long-term loans have different bases. The basis of the interest rate(s) on A.R.M. products is the INDEX it is tied to (e.g. the C.M.T., 11th District C.O.F.I., the L.I.B.O.R., the M.T.A.), on top of which the lender applies a [profit] MARGIN. Adding the index rate and the margin creates the "FULLY-INDEXED-RATE").

The basis of the interest rate on long-term fixed products, rather than an index, is the 'fixed' or stable 15, 20 and 30-year bond market. See "BONDS" above. (All things being equal, the difference in the monthly payment may change by roughly $20.00 - $40.00 per quarter point change in the interest rate for loan amounts up to $300,000.00, and somewhat higher for higher loan amounts). As an industry standard, interest rates are divided and expressed in eighth increments. The table below provides a breakdown and conversion of the interest rate scale.

INTEREST RATE CONVERSIONS

Fractions	Decimals	Terms
1/8	**0.125**	**One eighth**
¼	0.25	One quarter
3/8	**0.375**	**Three eighths**
½	0.5	One half
5/8	**0.625**	**Five eighths**
¾	0.75	Three quarters
7/8	**0.875**	**Seven eighths**
1	1	One point

JUMBO LOAN: ("JUMBO" as in a BIG loan amount). Though subject to change, by way of example, jumbo loans start(ed) at $417,650.00 on a Single Family Residence (i.e. 1 unit), $533,850 for 2 units, $645,300 for 3 units and $801,950 for 4 units on properties within the 48 contiguous united states, D.C. and P.R. A total loan amount less than $417,650.00 on an SFR is non-jumbo, or a "conforming" loan amount.

LESSEE: The person to whom property is rented or leased; otherwise, referred to as a "tenant" in most residential leases.

LESSOR: The person who rents or leases property to another. In residential leasing, such a person is called a landlord.

LIEN(S): An encumbrance (charge, liability) against property for money (voluntarily or involuntarily).

LIGHT OR ALTERNATE DOC': Lenders differ in criteria but as a rule, the qualification is half the requirement of Full Doc'.

LIS PENDENCE/PENDENS is something of an acronym or abbreviation of: Lawsuit IS PENDing. A pending lawsuit against a property negatively affects title. Lis Pendence is usually filed by a lender against a homeowner to commence the foreclosure process; however, it may also be filed by an opposing party against the homeowner to block the sale of the property - as a lawsuit/lien against property renders title unmarketable.

LOAN AMOUNT: In a refinance, the loan amount is expressed in two ways: the Base Loan Amount and the Total Loan Amount. The base loan amount includes the liens and debts to be paid off, cash-out, industry-standard, lender and/or broker-specific fees. The LTV is not calculated on the base loan amount, it is calculated on the total loan amount, which includes the same factors as the base loan amount *plus* the origination points. In a purchase money transaction, the total loan amount typically excludes points and fees, which are part of the non-recurring out-of-pocket closing costs borne by the buyer.

L.O.E. / L.O.X.: Letter of explanation.

A letter of explanation may be required and/or can help in matters of question with the lender, concerning employment tenure, late payments or other derogatory issues related to the credit profile or qualification.

L.T.V. (Loan To Value): The loan amount as compared to the property value percentage-wise; or the total loan amount divided by the property value. There are up to 7 LTV tiers of roughly 5 percentage points blocks, e.g.: 65%-70%, >70%-75%, >75%-80%, >80%-85%, >85%-90% >90%-95%, >95%-100%. (The difference between 100% of the property value and the lender's maximum Loan To Value is the % of the **Down Payment** required of the borrower; e.g. 80% L.T.V. = 20% D.P.). Most lenders stop at 95% LTV (especially for a single loan), and LTV below 65% is priced no differently and no better than the 65% level with most lenders. (See Loan To Value calculation in Mortgage Calculator Basics, section 6 below)

- Loan-To-Value so much as .001% higher than a given tier start level is priced at the top percent of that level (e.g. 70.001% LTV would be priced as 75% LTV. Conversely, loan-to-value a hair below a given tier start level is priced no higher than the start level of that range; e.g. 69.99% LTV would be priced as 65% LTV.

MARGIN (or "profit margin"): The difference between the index rate and the end or fully indexed (interest) rate of an ARM. INDEX + MARGIN = the "FULLY INDEXED" [Interest] Rate - on ARM products. Example: a 1.875% (index rate) plus a 4.0% (lender margin) equals a 5.875% "fully indexed" rate.

MOBILE/MANUFACTURED vs.
MODULAR/PRE-FABRICATED HOUSES:

A MOBILE OR "MANUFACTURED" home (called "mobile" [homes] prior to June 1976, and "manufactured" after June 1976) is built entirely at a factory and then transported to a site and installed there. The fact that the structure is made with or carried on wheels, (having an axle), classifies it as "mobile" (as it is moveable). Mobile/manufactured houses have a history of a high-loss/high default rate - as high as 12% - which is four times the default rate on conventional/site-built houses, making mobile/manufactured houses poor collateral. (In 2002, the largest lender on manufactured houses (Conseco Finance) was forced into bankruptcy after losing upwards of $4 billion in two years on such properties). Accordingly, mobile/manufactured houses are viewed and treated like unsecured or "personal" property - shunned by conventional lenders, who lend on "real" property. However, there are lenders that specialize in mobile/manufactured home financing and refinancing, but such lenders have qualifying requirements and limitations, such as doc' type (usu. full-doc' only), year-built cut-off dates (in consideration of environmental concerns such as asbestos levels, and observance of year-specific codes and regulations), structure size limits (e.g. not larger than a doublewide) etc. Another aspect that makes mobile/manufactured houses risky business for lenders is that about half of them are situated on short-term leased or rented land, where the decision of the house's permanency is at the discretion of the landowner. This is one of the primary reasons that lenders require that the homeowner own the land that the structure is situated on. Another reason land ownership is important is related to equity. Much of property appreciation or equity build-up is tied to rising land value, thus, if the land is not owned by the homeowner, their property enjoys little to no appreciation. On top of the homeowner owning the land on which their property sits (a "land-home" arrangement, as it may be called), lenders require that the structure be mounted/anchored/secured on a permanent foundation, to assure reasonable stability of the structure/investment against the possibility of natural disasters.

Crawl space: Mobile/manufactured Houses are usually placed upon a raised leveling/attachment system for the purpose of allowing access for structural inspection (to determine and report on the type and condition of attachments, e.g. plumbing, electrical, venting, ductwork etc; and to check for moisture intrusion or leakage). If a house has "crawl space", it is assumed to be a mobile/manufactured structure rather than site/stick-built house or even a modular/prefab'.

413/433 Certification: Manufactured/mobile homes that have had the wheels, axles, hitches and towing devices taken off and mounted on a permanent foundation may be classified "413" or "433" ("Permanent Foundation Certification"), signifying that the manufactured/mobile home, previously categorized as "personal" property, may be reclassified as "real" property.

Manufactured home - as defined in Section 18007 of the Health and Safety Code, is: "A structure (transportable in one or more sections) when in the traveling mode, is eight body feet or more in width, or 40 body feet or more in length, or, when erected on site, is 320 or more square feet. It is built on a permanent chassis and designed to be used as a dwelling with or without a permanent foundation when connected to the required utilities, and includes the plumbing, heating, air conditioning, and electrical systems contained therein" (H & S Code § 18007).

Manufactured/mobile homes are identified by HUD tags or DMV identification - not Assessor Parcel Numbers (which serve to identify parcels of land -- upon which structures sit). If a non-stick-built house was built after 6/15/76, a HUD tag may be found on the rear of such a structure, evincing it to be a Manufactured House, albeit built to HUD Standards & Safety Requirements. If a HUD tag cannot be found on a manufactured house, it was likely built before 6/15/76. HUD issued an amendment to the original description(s) of mobile homes in August of 1982, wherein it was determined that mobile homes built after June of 1976 would be referred to as "Manufactured Homes", and those built prior would yet be referred to as "mobile" (homes).

MODULAR/PRE-FABRICATED houses: Called "panelized" or "precut". Like mobile/manufactured houses, Modular/Pre-fab' units are built in a factory; however, they are assembled on the site (differing from mobile/manufactured structures that are assembled in a factory and installed or dropped-down on the site). Another marked difference is that modular/prefabricated houses are not built with or on wheels, have no axle and therefore are not "mobile" (moveable) homes; accordingly, many lenders will treated them like conventional S.F.R.'S. Most conventional lenders will not loan on mobile/manufactured houses but will loan on modular/prefabricated houses; however, in either case the house must be on a permanent foundation, and the land must be owned by the homeowner. (The "regular-type" of houses are called stick-built or site-built houses. See below).

MORTGAGE: The word mortgage was constructed from the Middle English word "morgage", which was derived from the Old French word "mort" - meaning "dead", as in the related word "morgue" - related to the Latin word "mortuus", the past participle of "mori", which means to die. The second half of the word mortgage, "gage", is another Middle English word, which means a pledge, pawn or security. The original concept came from the idea that a homeowner might not completely pay off the debt; thus the property was "gaged" or pledged as repayment of the loan against the possibility of the "mort" (death) or termination of payment from the borrower. By modern standards, the term mortgage is defined as: an interest in land created by a written instrument providing security for the performance of a duty or the payment of a debt. The mortgage is the document serving as evidence by which real estate is pledged as collateral for the repayment of a loan - otherwise called "HYPOTHECATION", which means: "to pledge to a creditor as security without delivering over". "To pledge property as security or collateral for a debt. Generally, there is no physical transfer of the pledged property to the lender, nor is the lender given title to the property; he has the right to sell the pledged property upon default".

NEG' AM' / Negative Amortization: This type of loan is designed so that the mortgage payment is less than the total interest due, and leaves the principle balance untouched. The unpaid interest portion of the mortgage payment is applied to the back of the loan (by the difference between the minimum payment rate and the fully-indexed rate), causing the ending balance of the loan to exceed the opening balance. This Negative Amortization is the opposite of "Positive Amortization" (i.e. P & I), which continually reduces the ending balance by steadily paying down the full principal and interest of the loan simultaneously. As with the Interest Only loan, the Neg' Am' loan is (to be) a short-term strategy, and of particular interest to first-time homebuyers (drawn by the low monthly payment), and to investors wanting to acquire property at minimal expense to convert it for maximum gain.

Negatively amortized loans are more handsomely referred to as "Deferred Interest" and "Minimum payment" loans.

- The CODI/COFI/COSI/LIBOR/MTA index-based Neg' Am' mortgage products are actually designed to pay the loan off as amortized by the end of the scheduled term, owing to the fluctuating dynamic and rate of 'rise' and 'reduction' in the loan balance, as naturally occurs over the course of time. All things being equal, eventually, these alternating periods offset each other and "wash-out", resulting in the mortgage being paid off at the length.

- There is an annual 7.5% maximum payment increase, designed to reach the full amount of interest due, which may take 6-8 years to occur, depending upon the initial starting rate, margin, and the movement of the operating index. The Lender will subtract the amount that exceeds the interest due from the principal balance, causing a reduction of the principal balance. Eventually, the annual 7.5% (maximum) payment increase will cause the minimum payments to reach the full P & I or scheduled payments.

51

- The limit may vary from lender to lender, but on average, the loan balance increase from the NEG' AM' payment (with an Option Arm) has a 110% maximum cap from the original loan balance in any 5-year period. If and when neg' am' payments cause the loan balance to reach the 110% limit, the lender will increase the minimum payment - without regard to the 7.5% payment cap - in order to facilitate the loan being paid off at the scheduled fully indexed rate and remaining term.

- On average, every five years, the lender "recasts" or re-amortizes the loan, adding the amount of deferred interest to the existing balance, and restructuring the loan as required in order to keep pace with the loan being paid off by the end of the original term.

N. E. V.: No Employment Verification performed.

N.I.N.A.: (No Income, No Asset verification; i.e. a true no-doc' loan): Employment, income and assets are not to be stated on the 1003 (only contact information listed), and no Debt Ratios calculated. (Credit score minimum and qualification(s) are set by the lender).

N. I. Q.: No Income Qualification.

N. I. V.: No Income Verification performed.

N.I.V.A. No Income, Verified Assets. Income is not stated (at all), no ratio(s) calculated; however, employment is stated on the 1003 and assets are verified. (Credit score minimum and qualification(s) determined by lender).

N.O.D. Notice Of Default: has reference to mortgage payment delinquency and is the stage prior to property foreclosure. As a rule an N.O.D. is recorded after mortgage payments have been in arrears or in "default" 90 days.

NO DOC' (was a sub-prime product): A loan in which no documentation of the borrower's income and/or assets is required. This differs from a stated-stated loan, which requires that income and assets at least be indicated on the 1003; however, the No Doc loan requires no indication of income or assets whatsoever but, a high credit score starting at 680 is normally required.

NON-OCCUPYING CO-BORROWER: As a rule or industry standard, a non-occupying co-borrower limits the L.T.V. of the loan to 95% if not less.

- If the non-occupying co-borrower owns (and occupies) another property and yet is portrayed as occupying the subject property (when in fact they do not), and the lender discovers it, the loan may be denied. If it is found out (through audit) after the loan has been done, the non-occupying co-borrower may be forced sell their other property to retain the subject property.

NON-RECURRING CLOSING COSTS: Those costs factored into the loan that occur one time; costs that do not repeat, e.g. the cost of appraisal, doc' drawing, escrow and title, notary, odd-days interest, processing, origination and rebate points, wire transfer, etc. In a sale, the seller of a property may concede to the buyer (called a making a "concession" or a "contribution" of) 3%-6% of the appraised property value toward the buyer's closing costs to defray the buyer's financial burden. The buyer is responsible for providing the required amount that may exceed the seller's permissible contribution.

"ODD DAYS" INTEREST: Projected interest. In a refinance situation, interest is packed into the loan amount by both the old and the new lender. The payoff demand from the old lender will reflect the interest due on the existing loan (to the date specified), and the new lender will exact a per diem rate of interest for up to 30 days (as indicated on the 1003/G.F.E.). Should the loan close before the number of days indicated, the borrower will receive the overage as cash back, but should the loan close after the number of days indicated, the borrower will be "short-to-close". As such, the borrower will have to pay the unpaid interest - from the cash-out, if any, or out-of-pocket at the signing table.

ORIGINATION POINT(S) (also called "up-front" points): Each origination point equals 1% of the loan amount and determines the L.O.'s commission on a mortgage loan. The normal range of points charged front-to-backend (i.e., origination and rebate) is 1%-5%.

PAR (RATE): The basic interest rate - without rebate/back-end points.

PAYOFF DEMAND: Shows the current balance due on the mortgage, and shows whether or not there is a prepayment penalty. Obtaining the payoff demand is mandatory. It is the document that the lender relies on to determine the true current mortgage balance/payoff amount.

PER ANNUM (Latin): Per year / Annually

PER DIEM (Latin): Per day / Daily

PERSONAL PROPERTY: In a broad and general sense, everything that is the subject of ownership, not coming under the denomination of real estate. Also referred to as "CHATTEL", meaning: effects or property that are tangible and movable, differing from "real" property or "real estate", which is land and anything permanently affixed thereto (e.g. buildings and those things attached to buildings, such as plumbing, heating fixtures, light fixtures, fences and other such items or structures that would be personal property if not attached). Title to personal property is transferred via a bill of sale, while real property is transferred by way of a deed instrument.

PIGGYBACK (second): The second position lien of a combination loan - such as the 20% loan of an 80%/20% combo'. "Second's" that are not "piggyback"/combo seconds are called "stand alone" seconds, which are not widely popular with mortgage lenders because the small loan amounts provide little remuneration and gratification to the lender for the work required to do them. Although the piggyback second-position lien is tied to the greater first-position lien, lenders may also charge a fee to do the piggyback second that is separate from the fee(s) charged to do the first position lien.

P.M.I. (Private Mortgage Insurance): With conventional mortgages, PMI is typical at >80% L.T.V. This is an additional cost to the borrower for having a "high-risk" L.T.V. and compensates the lender for taking the risk. PMI payment is insurance for the lender against the possibility of the borrower failing to pay on the loan. A combination loan with the first position lien being 80% or less is preferable to a single loan at greater than 80% LTV for the purpose of avoiding PMI. Also, the combination second lien has tax deductibility, whereas PMI is not tax deductible. Following are PMI factors:

Average PMI max. factors on 30-year (fixed) mortgages:

- 80.01 to 85% LTV, the PMI factor is 0.0032 (or .32%) of the loan amount, divided by 12.

- 85.01 to 90% LTV, the PMI factor is 0.0052 (or .52%) of the loan amount, divided by 12.

- 90.01 to 95% LTV, the PMI factor is 0.0078 (or .78%) of the loan amount, divided by 12.

- 95.01 to 97% LTV, the PMI factor is 0.009   (or   .9%) of the loan amount, divided by 12.

<u>Average PMI max. factors on 15-year (fixed) mortgages</u>:

- 80.01 to 85% LTV, the PMI factor is .0021 (or .21%) of the loan amount, divided by 12.

- 85.01 to 90% LTV, the PMI factor is .0023 (or .23%) of the loan amount, divided by 12.

- 90.01 to 95% LTV, the PMI factor is .0056 (or .56%) of the loan amount, divided by 12.

- 95.01 to 97% LTV, the PMI factor is .0079 (or .79%) of the loan amount, divided by 12.

For mortgage loans of > 80% LTV where PMI has been applied, the borrower may (and should) request termination of their PMI when the LTV of their original mortgage balance drops to 80% or less, but which may take a number of years to happen if the loan is paid according to the amortization schedule.

P & I: A Principle and Interest [only] mortgage payment; otherwise referred to as: "Unimpounded".

PITI: A mortgage payment including Principle and Interest plus Taxes and Insurance; otherwise called: "Impounded".

P.O.C.: Paid Outside of Closing: A cost that is not covered in the loan and is paid outside of escrow or out-of-pocket by the borrower, e.g. the appraisal fee, which is usually paid to the appraiser by the borrower at the door.

P.O.I. Proof Of "Income" (paystubs, W-2's 1099's, etcetera).

PORTFOLIO (LENDER): A lender that processes, keeps and services their loans rather than selling them on the secondary market or to servicing companies; as such, the structure of portfolio-lender loans may not, nor have to conform to Freddie Mac and Fannie Mae standards. Not being bound by secondary market limitations allows Portfolio Lenders greater flexibility with program guidelines and discretion that banks beholden to the secondary market can't offer.

POWER-OF-ATTORNEY: A document serving to deputize a person, called the "attorney-in-fact", to act as the agent on behalf of another, as per the terms of the agreement, expressed in writing. An attorney-in-fact would be a competent but disinterested party who is authorized by another person to act in their stead. Particularly in real estate conveyance transactions, an attorney-in-fact, (having a fiduciary obligation to his or her principal), should be officially authorized by a written, notarized and recordable instrument to substantiate such granting of authority. Typically implemented on a limited if not an isolated basis.

PREPAID FINANCE CHARGE(S) (PFC): Prepaid Finance Charges are certain charges made in connection with the loan that must be agreed to be paid or financed through the loan (through escrow, at the close of the loan), such as reserves, interest, title insurance, escrow fees, origination, discount points and other *non-recurring* charges.

PREPAYMENT PENALTY: (Typical for sub-prime, exceptional for prime). A prepayment penalty is a financial penalty (roughly 80% of the loan balance or 2%-3% of the opening loan amount, or 5 or 6 months of the interest portion of the mortgage payment. This penalty is applied to a loan to discourage the early payoff or refinance of a mortgage. The prepayment penalty serves to insure both the profitability and stability of the investment for the secondary market investors (FNMA, FHLMC, etc.) who buy the loans from the lenders and in doing so, replenish the lenders' "warehouse line" of money to fund future loans.

- The longer the pre-pay', the lower the interest rate, the shorter the 'prepay', the higher the interest rate. The duration of the prepayment penalty on an A.R.M. is usually commensurate with the fixed period (usually 2-3 years, and normally not exceeding five years). On long-term "fixed" loans, the P.P.P. period is usually three years in duration.

- The P.P.P. can be reduced or waived altogether – at a cost. The prepayment penalty is not an out-of-pocket expense and is tax-deductible in the year it is paid as "itemized interest" (being deemed prepaid or accelerated interest).

- Hard Prepay: With a hard prepay', in the event that the homeowner sells their property, they would have to incorporate the prepayment penalty into the loan. The Hard Prepay, however, offers a better interest rate than the Soft Prepay, to raise its appeal.

- Soft Prepay: With a soft prepay', in the event that a homeowner sells their property, they would not have to incorporate the prepayment penalty into the loan. The Soft Prepay, however, results in a higher interest rate than the Hard Prepay to lessen its appeal. (Raising the interest rate effectively works to pay the PPP in a soft prepay situation). A soft prepayment penalty automatically converts to a hard prepayment penalty in a refinance transaction.

PRIMARY BORROWER: As a rule, in a borrower/co-borrower situation, the primary borrower is the individual who earns the most money – not the individual with the higher credit score.

PRIME RATE: The prime rate, as defined by the Wall Street Journal, is: "The base rate on corporate loans posted by at least 75% of the nation's 30 largest banks". The rate is typically the same among the major banks and adjustments to the prime rate are made by the banks uniformly.

The prime rate does not adjust on any regular basis and is not very volatile; however, when it rises, it generally does so quickly, and then declines very slowly.

- The prime rate changes when the nation's largest banks decide together to raise or lower their base rate. The rate may not change for years, but then it has also changed several times in a single year. The PRIME interest RATE on loans is offered by banks to their high-credit-score/low-risk clients.

- Only a small percentage of customers qualify for the prime rate - which serves as a basis for the criteria of higher risk loan models. The prime rate is the prevailing bond rate, which, when combined with the lender's margin, creates the fully indexed rate. "Sub-prime" on the other hand is as much as 3% or higher than prime rate.

P.T.D. "Prior To Doc's": Conditions to be met prior to documents being drawn for signing.

P.T.F. Prior To Funding: Lender stipulations that must be satisfied before the loan can be funded.

PROPERTY CLASSIFICATIONS: There are essentially three types of property: Primary Residence (or: Owner Occupied), Investment Property (or: Non Owner Occupied/Rental), and Second Home (occasional or seasonal occupancy by owner but neither a rental nor primary residence). Property may be vested any number of ways (see "vesting" below) but basically speaking, property will be held as Individual/Single, with a Spouse or Other.

QUITCLAIM DEED (not "Quick-claim" deed): By legal definition, a quitclaim deed is: "A deed of conveyance operating by way of release; that is intended to pass any title, interest or claim which the grantor may have in the premises, but not professing that such title is valid, nor containing any warranty or covenants for title." However, in more recent and practical use, the quitclaim deed has been used more loosely for the simple purpose of adding or removing a party's interest in real property.

A quitclaim deed may be used where a deeding party (the grantor), having ownership interest in a property, quits or relinquishes their (sole) claim to (their) property and extends, vests or grants ownership/shared interest/holding power in the subject property to another (the grantee). This differs from a GRANT DEED, which is used to transfer the [real] property itself. A quitclaim deed can also be used to remedy certain problems with a title; for example, if there is a "cloud" or "defect" on the title, meaning that the current owner is not the only person with ownership rights in the property, the matter can be corrected by the previous (other) owner signing a quitclaim deed, transferring all of their rights in the property to the current owner.

- Although an individual in a co-borrower situation that is on a loan and shares responsibility for the mortgage note can be quitclaimed or "deeded-off" title they may not be quitclaimed off or otherwise released from liability for the mortgage note/payment as long as the loan is in force.

- In the event that a borrower wants to refinance and use a co-borrower that is not on title, they can have the co-borrower quitclaimed onto title (which may take thirty or more days to reflect); however, absent the required seasoning and proof of "vested interest" (see below) in the property, such a person may not be eligible to be a co-borrower.

RATE & TERM: In a "rate and term" refinance loan, the borrower's only concern is getting a lower interest rate and/or improved term on their property, expressing no interest in getting cash-out, consolidating debt or anything else.

REAL PROPERTY: "Land, and generally whatever is erected or growing upon or affixed to land." The earth's surface, the space above and the ground below, as well as all appurtenances to the land including buildings, structures, fixtures, fences and improvements erected upon or affixed to the same, excluding growing crops.

REBATE POINT (also called "back-end", "buy-up" or "Yield Spread"/YSP points): A commission point (like an origination point) applied to the back of the loan, that gets absorbed into the interest rate, causing it to increase - typically by half of a point (.50) per each rebate point applied. Prime lenders tend to have the rebate adjustment built in to their pricing table (interest rate sheet), however, sub-prime lenders do not, thus the A. E. (the lender's Account Executive) and the L. O. (Loan Officer) must manually adjust the rate according to the lender's ratio.

RECORDATION: The recording of an instrument (document), such as a deed or mortgage in a public registry.

RECURRING CLOSING COSTS: The costs of a loan that repeat (monthly) throughout the life of the loan, including: Insurance, Interest and Taxes.

RENTAL PROPERTY: Only 75% of gross rent from rental property is calculated for loan (income) qualification. The residual 25% of the gross rent monies represents the cost factor (regular maintenance/upkeep and vacancy) for the property owner.

RENT-BACK: A "rent-back" is a situation where a homeowner in a distressed situation (e.g. N.O.D. or foreclosure) is bought out by another party who allows the ex-homeowner to remain in the property, paying "rent back" to the new owner. The idea is to give the previous homeowner the grace and ability to redeem the property in the future. This is a potentially good situation for homeowners in distressed situations with good equity in their property, as the equity may be set aside as reserves (up to a year's-worth) to make sure that (with discipline) there is money on hand to make the house payments on time for a full year. This provides a manageable way for the residing ex-homeowner to establish a clean 12-month mortgage payment history, improving the ex-homeowner's credit profile and ability to redeem the property.

R.E.O.: Real Estate Owned - but owned by the bank or lender rather than the buyer/borrower. In other words, it is real estate that has been repossessed; consequently, it also called a "bank repo'". It is also referred to as a "settled" transaction.

RESERVES: Funds set aside for the purpose of insuring the payment of future obligations or claims.

R.E.S.P.A.: Real Estate Settlement Procedures Act: a consumer protections statute related to closing costs and settlement procedures - enforced by H.U.D. This statute regulates timely and accurate disclosure(s) of information to consumers related to their mortgage transaction.

RETAIL LENDER: Direct lender (as opposed to a Broker).

REVENUE: Gross income less operating expenses. To the Loan Officer being paid on "revenue", this means that their commission split (with the office) will be based on what is left after operating expenses have been deducted from the total income yield of the loan. The total "income" yield from a loan includes all fees that "profit" the office, e.g. processing, administrative, application fee(s), origination and rebate points. Example: if a loan yields $5,000.00 in total or gross income to the office, and the office claims $1,500.00 of the income to cover operating expenses, the balance of $3,500.00 is the "revenue" and amount that the commission-split may be based on, not the $5,000.00 amount.

REVERSE MORTGAGE: The Department of Housing and Urban Development implemented reverse mortgages as a way for senior citizen homeowners to keep from losing their homes, and from which, to derive financial support.

- Mortgages that are paid down or paid 'forward' from the time of financing or refinancing until paid off, are forward mortgages that over time, reduces debt and increases equity. Conversely the "Reverse Mortgage", rather than being paid down or forward by the homeowner pays the homeowner -- in reverse of the norm, which, over time, reduces equity and increases debt. In a forward mortgage, "income" is leveraged for equity. In a reverse mortgage equity is leveraged for "income".

- A reverse mortgage can provide a low-risk way for seniors (min. age limit: 62) who may have a lot of equity but little "income" to not only avoid losing their home but remain in it 'rent-free' so-to-speak, and moreover, to receive tax-free cash advances for the balance of their lives, to be used at their discretion, for daily living expenses, medical bills, retirement, travel, home improvement, etc. However, the homeowner remains responsible for property upkeep, property taxes and keeping current property insurance.

- The amount of money that the borrower can receive and how they receive it (e.g. lump sum, line of credit, fixed monthly stipends or a combination of either) is based on qualifying factors, such as age, program type, property value, locale, and current interest rate(s).

There have been 4 types of Reverse Mortgage plans:

1. The "H.E.C.M." (Home Equity Conversion Mortgage): the oldest and most popular reverse mortgage product on the market (since 1989), accounts for more than 90% of the total reverse mortgage market share. HECM loans are insured by the FHA which is part of HUD. Of the reverse mortgage programs that have been available, the HECM is the only one insured by the federal government. The H.E.C.M. reverse mortgage product is not equity-based but eligibility-based. Because the loan's viability is not contingent on equity, the borrower does not lose upon equity depletion. As the HECM is insured by the Federal Housing Authority, there are no negative repercussions to the borrower should the property experience negative equity. Should negative equity exist at the time the homeowner passes, the proceeds of the sale of the property and FHA insurance pays off the loan.

2. The Fannie Mae "Home Keeper" & "Home Keeper for Home Purchase" mortgage: Developed as a proprietary product of Fannie Mae in 1996.

Designed (as an alternative) to supplement the federally insured HECM's, by addressing the unmet needs that could not be served by the HECM program, embracing individuals with higher property values, condominium owners, and seniors wishing to use a reverse mortgage to purchase a new home. The interest rate on the "Home Keeper" product is adjustable, but may never rise by more than 12 percentage points above the initial rate; there is no cap on monthly adjustments other than the lifetime cap. (Fannie Mae is also a major investor in the HECM secondary market).

3. The Financial Freedom "Cash Account" loan: A proprietary jumbo reverse mortgage product introduced several years ago by the Financial Freedom Senior Funding Corporation (out of Irvine, CA), to benefit homeowners living in higher-priced homes valued above the FHA and Fannie Mae lending limits. This loan is offered by most reverse mortgage lenders. (Financial Freedom is/was a subsidiary of IndyMac Bank, F.S.B. "Proprietary" reverse mortgages, such as the Fannie Mae and IndyMac Bank products above are private loans which are backed by the companies that develop them).

4. Single-purpose reverse mortgages, which are offered by some state and local government agencies and nonprofit organizations, are purpose-specific, limiting the qualification and use of the monies borrowed. As a loan, and as a rule, reverse mortgages are required to be repaid in full (cash advances plus interest) upon the decease of the last surviving homeowner or sale of the property, whereupon the borrower(s) or their heirs would only receive the monies left from the proceeds after the mortgage has been paid off. If the property sells for less than the outstanding balance of the loan, the lender takes a loss. The reverse mortgage is a "non-recourse limit" loan, which means that the lender does not have legal recourse to anything other than the home's value when seeking repayment of the loan, nor may the lender seek repayment from the borrower's income, other assets, or heirs.

No matter how much the loan balance increases, neither the borrowers nor their inheriting heirs ever owe more than the property's fair market value.

Repayment of the loan also becomes due when:

- Homeowner fails to pay property taxes and/or keep current hazard insurance or violates any other stipulated borrower obligation(s).

- Any period the borrower or last surviving borrower no longer occupies the home as their principal residence, having permanently vacated the property by failing to reside there for twelve consecutive months.

- The homeowner allows the property to deteriorate (except for reasonable wear and tear), and fails to correct the problem(s).

As with anything, a reverse mortgage has pros and cons, and thus, should not be entered into unadvisedly.

A reverse mortgage counselor should be consulted who can explain the differences, benefits and cautions of the several types of programs available and determine which is best for the circumstances and goals of the borrower.

Reverse mortgages may have fixed or variable rates. Interest on reverse mortgages is not tax deductible until the loan is sufficiently paid down or paid off. The reverse mortgage may be repaid in full at any time; however, if payment in full is made within 36 months of advanced funds, a pre-payment penalty amount will be assessed and an interest rate differential payment may also be required. The penalty however will be waived if the reverse mortgage is repaid as a result of the death of the last surviving spouse - or reduced if the reverse mortgage is repaid as a result of the long-term medical care and/or institutionalization of the last surviving spouse.

HEIRS: If the loan ends due to the death of the last surviving borrower, the loan must be repaid before the home's title can be transferred to the borrower's heirs. The heirs do not necessarily have to sell the property to repay the debt, though they may. elect to do so. Repayment may be accomplished by refinancing the reverse mortgage into a traditional "forward mortgage" loan, or with the borrower's own funds or other funds from the borrower's estate, or with other assets.

If, at the end of the loan, the balance is less than the value of the home (or the net sale proceeds if sold), the borrower or their heirs get the difference - after the amount owed to the lender is repaid. The lender does not get the house - they do not want the house - they want the repayment of the loan. Again - because reverse mortgages are typically "non [legal] recourse" loans - if, at the end of the loan, the balance exceeds the property's market value, the borrower or their heirs are not liable for any amount above the market value of the property- the lender takes a loss - not the borrower(s).

ROLLING LATE(S): A payment grid reflecting the same numerically coded payment delinquency in repeating or consecutive or "rolling" fashion. Late payments that are non-rolling have a different numeric value between them. Example of a rolling late: 113<u>222</u>X<u>221</u>X2. Example of non-rolling late's: 1231X2X3X411. (1 signifies timely payments. 2 signifies 30 days late. 3 signifies 60 days late. 4 signifies 90 days late. 5 signifies 120 days late. 6 signifies N.O.D status. An X or dash – mark signifies a non-reported payment or a payment made late but <30 days late). There is usually a limit to the number of rolling late's that a lender will accept.

"SALLIE MAE" (SLM Corp.): The Student Loan Marketing Association: the largest provider of federally insured educational loans in the U.S.

SEASONING: Signifying "how long". The duration, length or "season" of time related to a concern, such as funds, occupancy, periods between refinancing etc.

SECOND MORTGAGE: As a rule, second mortgages do not have prepayment penalties applied and do not include taxes and insurance in the payment unless requested by the borrower. The amortization term of a second mortgage (e.g. 20/20, 30/15, 30/30, with or without an I/O option) is critical to specify, as it determines the monthly payment.

SECONDARY MARKET: Mortgage loans created between the borrower and the lender occur in or on the "primary" market. There is also a "secondary market" wherein and whereby the lender can recoup the funds that they lent to the borrower by selling the same loan to outside investors.

Mortgages that have been funded are pooled together with other loans of like rate and term, which group of loans in turn are packaged as a M.B.S.'s (Mortgage Backed Securities) to be sold to investors (like the twin titans Fannie Mae and Freddie Mac, who set the guidelines and underwriting standards for the loans that they buy). M.B.S. pools can also be comprised of loans that do not fit Fannie and Freddie guidelines (e.g. Jumbo loans that are bought by hedge funds or private investors). Presently, the investor of over 90% of mortgages in America is the federal government via FHA and VA loans, Freddie Mac and Fannie Mae.

The "servicing rights" of a loan (where the investor pays a "servicer" - typically one of the larger banks - for "collecting" the loan payments) may be sold also as a separate action, different from the loan itself being sold to an investor - who receives the interest on their purchase of the loan. While the second bank purchases the servicing rights of the loan, they did not finance the full amount; that again, came from the secondary/investor market.

An investor makes more on a higher rate mortgage backed security, but which is considered more likely to pay off early by a refinance. A mortgage with a lower rate that pays the investor less is nonetheless more likely to remain stable to the loan's maturity, and being less likely to be paid off early, is considered a more valuable asset to the loan servicer, who loses the fee income from the investor when the loan pays off.

Mortgage rates and fees are driven by competition and risk among private investors on the secondary market. Loans that are perceived as risky (e.g. borrowers with low credit scores and higher interest rates) forces fees being charged designed to attract investors. Mortgage rates are the middle ground between what the borrower can afford to pay for their loan and what investors are willing to settle for as a return on their investment. After the subprime mortgage bubble burst, investors became leery of investing in M.B.S.'s with low rates, whereupon the government acted to fill the void in the secondary mortgage market to restrain interest rates from reaching a pitch that hardly anyone could afford, effectively killing the housing market and connected investment community.

SECURED LOAN: A loan that is tied to real property (or some physical or financial asset), the value of which is guaranteed by the pledge or collateral of such property or asset. A secured loan, one backed by assets belonging to the borrower that may be forfeited to the lender should the borrower fail to pay the loan. The "security" makes the loan a low-risk proposition to the lender. A secured loan is also referred to as a "note loan" or "signature loan". (An "unsecured" loan by contrast is a loan that is granted and supported merely by a borrower's apparent creditworthiness, rather than by an asset or some sort of collateral").

SECURITIZATION: A Lender's ("warehouse") line of credit or capital, with which loans can be financed/funded.

The money for "securitization" in large part comes from loans that are sold by lenders on the secondary market to investors (e.g. Fannie Mae, Freddie-Mac, insurance companies, private investors, etc).

SELLER CONCESSION: When the seller concedes or credits the purchaser a certain amount of the appraised value of the subject property to cover the non-recurring closing costs (fees and points), reducing or eliminating the borrower having to pay the same out of pocket. The "seller concession" (typically 3%-6%) is to be stipulated in the purchase agreement. When the appraised value of the subject property exceeds the initial purchase price, the seller may elect to contribute the excess to the buyer to assist with the non-recurring closing costs, as the lender may permit. Another way the seller can make a contribution is to reduce the asking price so that there is enough remaining (between the asking price and the appraised value) to pay for the closing costs the seller agrees to cover.

S.F.R.: Single Family Residence. A residential structure designed to house a single family: a "one-unit" dwelling (as opposed two to four unit dwellings).

SHORT SALE (also called "pre-foreclosure" property): When a property sells short of the balance owed on it, often done to avoid the blight of foreclosure but which does not necessarily relieve the borrower of the obligation to pay the remaining balance of the loan if the proceeds from the sale of the property do not cover it; also called a "deficiency [judgment]". A lender may also consider a short sale even though the borrower is not delinquent, in the event the property value falls, resulting in the seller owing more than the property is worth.

SHORT-TO-CLOSE: When the borrower owes money outside of the loan.

Being short-to-close is when the borrower has to come up with monies out of pocket in order to close/complete the transaction, rather than breaking even or getting cash-out of the loan.

SILENT SECOND: A loan/lien on a property granted by a municipality that does not need to be paid down or paid off unless the mortgage is sold or refinanced; thus, it is referred to as a "silent" second. It is called a second, because it is an additional lien on the property, subordinate to the 1st position lien/mortgage. A silent second may or may not appear on a borrower's credit report but normally appears on the title report. A portion of the property's equity may be claimed by the municipality providing the silent second upon the sale or refinance of the property, resulting in the borrower paying on the "back end" for the privilege of having a silent second.

S.I.S.A. Stated Income Stated Assets (also called "Stated-Stated"). Employment, earnings and assets are stated on the 1003 (but assets are not verified) and debt ratios are calculated.

S.I.V.A. Stated Income Verified Assets. Employment and monthly earnings are to be noted on the 1003, assets are verified and ratios are calculated. (Qualification(s) for S.I.V.A. may vary from lender to lender).

SOURCING: Signifying the source of funds/monies being provided for the loan, e.g., checking, savings, a gift, etc.

STATED INCOME/STATED DOC': Where the borrower simply states their income and does not have to verify or document it (beyond the 1003 information). The lender will accept the stated "income" as long as it is within reason for the related profession. Although the borrower's "income" will not be verified, their employment will be (V.O.E.).

In a stated income loan, the income to be stated is reasonably flexible and may be adjusted for Debt Ratio purposes (again, as long as the amount stated is within the acceptable range for the related profession, increasing the stated income may be acceptable). As a rule, in either full doc' or stated scenarios, it is not the party with the highest credit score but the party (between co-borrowers) who earns the most money that qualifies as the "primary borrower". Typically, a loan that is originally submitted as STATED may be converted to FULL DOC' (*but not vice-versa*); in such a case, the loan would have to be withdrawn from the lender and appropriately resubmitted to another lender.

STICK-BUILT/SITE-BUILT [HOUSES]: A house that is built brick-by-brick, so-to-speak or [stick] piece by [stick] piece on or at the designated site (hence the term: "site-built"). This type of house differs from mobile/manufactured and modular structures, which are for the most part made in a factory and then transported to the designated site for installation or assembly.

SUBJECT PROPERTY: The property targeted for refinance or purchase.

SUBMISSION: Required documents submitted for underwriting approval. A complete submission package includes five or six things, such as: The 1003 (loan application), 1008 (Transmittal Summary), credit report, appraisal, Preliminary Report and earnings or "income" documentation when applicable.

SUBORDINATION: When a lender ordinally ahead or positionally in front of another lender agrees to take a subordinate or posterior position to another lender (e.g. a lender that was in first position agrees to take second position - behind another lender). Lenders do not favor subordinating because their pay priority ranking drops with their position.

TITLE: The (instrument/document) evidence that one has right of possession of land. The fact of possessing or the legal right to take possession of something: A legal document evincing a person's right to or ownership of a property; as such, a title is the foundation of property ownership, differing from a deed. A deed is essentially a document by which the interest or right(s) of ownership in real property is transferred. A deed is not necessarily or by itself proof of ownership and does not annul the rights others may have in the property. Additionally, a deed will not show liens or claims that may be outstanding against the title (which a title report shows).

TITLE SEARCH/PRELIMINARY REPORT: A title search or "Prelim'" is an examination of all public records that involve the title to a specific property. The search is conducted to reveal any defects: to verify that there are no liens or other claims against the property other than those targeted to be cleared at closing, if done for a purchase. A title search uncovers any "cloud" on title: whether or not all former owners have formally given up their rights to the property. The search looks for and looks at past owners and deeds, wills, trusts, mortgages, judgments, and other encumbrances against the property. Title searches typically include documents filed during the past 30 years.

TITLE INSURANCE: Title insurance is protection against claims against a property, and will, to the extent provided for in the policy, provide for legal defense and pay court costs and related fees, and where a claim proves valid, provide for the reimbursement for actual loss, up to the face amount of the policy for the insured.

- Lenders require a title insurance policy on all mortgage loans that they issue to protect the loan (and the lender) against the cost of settling any disputes that may arise. The homeowner should also acquire title insurance for protection against problems that were not identified in the title search. The homeowner's title insurance amount is usually equivalent to the property's value and lasts as long as the owner maintains a financial interest in the property.

- ALTA & CLTA: In California, there are usually two policies of title insurance issued in connection with finance and refinance transactions: "ALTA" (American Land Title Association) and "CLTA" (California Land Title Association) policies. The policies are not identical. An ALTA policy generally provides broader coverage than a CLTA policy, thus, it may appear that the Lender obtains better coverage than the Buyer. In particular, CLTA policies usually exclude coverage for boundary disputes. An ALTA policy is the type of insurance normally procured by the Lender to insure its interest in the title to the real property, which also stands as security for the loan. A CLTA policy is the type often obtained by Buyers to insure their interest in the title to the property conveyed to them by the Sellers. The CLTA Owner's Policy insures all recorded matters affecting title to the property in order of their priority, such as reflecting the lender of the first mortgage before the lender on the second mortgage.

- Title insurance involves a one-time premium, paid at the close of a real estate transaction and provides coverage only for that specific transaction. Title insurance guarantees that the title company has thoroughly searched and evaluated the condition of the title to a property, and guarantees that no items were missed which may affect the property; that all events in the past related to the property have been cleared, so that no claims will ever arise; however, title insurance safeguards against the possibility of discrepancies, errors or omissions in the title search. A percentage of title companies' profits are reserved for the payment of claims that may arise.

- Most title companies will insure a seller carry-back deed of trust under an ALTA residential policy by endorsement (an addendum to a title policy with a small additional cost) and is the only buyer-type deed of trust that may be insured under an ALTA policy.

TORT [LAW]: The body or branch of law dealing with the adjudication and remedy of civil infractions. The word TORT comes from the Latin word *tortious*, meaning: "wrong", but in relation to real estate, applies to civil (rather than criminal) wrongful actions done to a person or property (excepting breach of contract), intentionally, unintentionally or by negligence.

- Tort law is designed to award the injured party financial compensation from the injuring party for damages, so that they (the injuring party) will likewise suffer pain caused by their action(s).

TRADE LINES/LINE OF CREDIT: A trade line is simply another terminology for a *loan* that reflects on a credit report with a payment history. There are open and closed trade lines of credit. Each lender has their own criteria concerning trade line qualification(s).

TRUST: A fiduciary (financial) relationship under which, one is trusted or entrusted to hold property, real or personal, for the benefit of another.

TRUSTEE: (1) One who is appointed or required by law to execute a trust. (2) One who holds legal title to real property "in trust" for the benefit of another person (beneficiary), and who owes a fiduciary duty to the beneficiary.

UNIMPOUNDED: A mortgage payment that does not include taxes and insurance (only Principal and Interest).

UNDERWRITE: A sum of money contributed (by underwriter) to an activity undertaken by others, guaranteed to compensate for any loss or deficiency from the undertaking.

Capital put up to finance a business venture and agreement to assume liability to the extent specified in terms.

VA LOANS (Department of **V**eterans **A**dministration): The VA was established under the "Servicemen's Readjustment Act", passed by congress in 1944 with the intent of providing home financing for eligible veterans in areas or cases where private financing may not be available without a down payment. Like the FHA, the VA does not lend money to borrowers but rather creates and manages the guidelines by which VA-approved lending institutions (such as banks, savings & loan and mortgage companies) provide VA loans. Also, as with the FHA - the government - that is, the VA "guarantees", "insures" or protects the lender - not the borrower - against loss, should the borrower default on the loan, which replaces what the lender normally receives by requiring a down payment (again, is not required with VA loan).

VA loans are for eligible military veterans - those with honorable discharge - and active duty personnel who qualify in full time service as a member of the Army, Navy, Air Force, Marine Corps, Coast Guard (and even a commissioned officer of the public health service, environmental administration or the national oceanic and atmospheric administration), who can prove their eligibility with forms DD-214, DD-215 or a WD form for WWII vets, documenting their full name, military service number, branch of service, dates of service and type of discharge.

- While the VA does not require a down payment on home purchases up to $417,000 in California, a private lender, in exceptional cases, may require a down payment; also, if the purchase price is more than the reasonable value of the property, a down payment may be required. And while a down payment as a rule is not required in a VA purchase loan, expenses over and above the price of the property must be provided for or absorbed by the buyer and/or seller.

(e.g., the 3.3% funding fees - required by law and other closing costs - which are comparable with other financing standards and procedures). Other VA features and benefits include:

- Lenient income and credit qualifying standards.
- Up to 100% "straight" LTV loan for home purchases
- Up to 90% LTV for home refi's
- No seasoning of home ownership required for refinancing VA loans
- No PMI
- No Prepayment Penalty
- Cash-out up to $144,000
- Bk's >2 years may be disregarded by lenders
- Seller contributions toward closing costs up to 4% of the purchase price
- The mortgage payment may be up to 41% of the buyer's gross "income", compared to the near 30% limit with conventional mortgage products
- Jumbo (VA) loans in given areas up to $729,000.00.
- VA loans are assumable
- VA loans are and must be "Impounded"
- Owner Occupancy is required
- In the event the veteran dies, the loan must still be *re*paid by the surviving spouse or other co-borrower

VENDOR: The seller of realty.

VESTED INTEREST: A personal and/or financial stake one has in an asset, transaction or security. "A present right or title to a thing...One in which there is a present fixed right, either of present enjoyment or of future enjoyment" (Black's Law Dic., 6th Ed.). A party that is not on the mortgage note but is on title and can evince that they in fact have been paying the mortgage (e.g. with up to twelve months of cancelled checks as proof) may be granted "vested interest" in a property, being the payor in fact.

VESTING: The manner in which a property will be held (i.e. ownership status), and as it will be reflected on title. Following is list of common types of ownership and co-ownership:

- A SINGLE MAN/WOMAN: A man or woman who has never been [legally] married; in which case, vesting would read: John Q, a single man / Jane Q a single woman.

- AN UNMARRIED MAN/WOMAN: A man or woman, who is legally divorced, for whom vesting would read: John Q, an unmarried man / Jane Q, an unmarried woman.

- SOLE AND SEPARATE PROPERTY: When a married man or woman intends to acquire title in his or her name only; however, the spouse must consent by evidence of an instrument (quitclaim deed or otherwise) to the transfer, thereby relinquishing all right, title and interest in the property. In such case, vesting would read: John Q, a married man (or Jane Q, a married woman), as His/Her Sole and Separate Property.

- COMMUNITY PROPERTY: As defined in the California Civil Code is: "Property acquired by a husband and wife, or either, during marriage, when not acquired as the separate property of either. Real estate conveyed to a married man or woman is presumed to be community property, unless otherwise indicated. Either spouse has the right to dispose of one half of the community property by will. If there is no will however, the property will be left to the surviving spouse without administration. If a spouse exercises his/her right to dispose of one-half of the property, that half is subject to administration in the estate." In such cases, vesting may read: John Q & Jane Q, husband and wife, as community property; or: John Q & Jane Q, husband and wife.

- COMMUNITY PROPERTY WITH RIGHT OF SURVIVORSHIP: This vesting bears the same characteristics as the traditional community property form of title, with addition of the right of survivorship, as with "Joint Tenancy";

i.e., when a husband and wife hold title as Community Property with Right of Survivorship the full interest in the property will vest, by law, in the surviving spouse immediately upon the death of their spouse.

- JOINT TENANTS: As defined in the California Civil Code, a Joint Tenancy estate is a joint interest owned by two or more persons in equal shares, by a title created by a single will or transfer, when expressly declared in the will or transfer to be joint tenancy. A salient characteristic of joint tenancy property is the right of survivorship. Upon the decease of either tenant, title to the property will immediately vest in the surviving joint tenant(s). As a consequence, joint tenancy property is not subject to disposition by will. In such case, vesting would read: John Q and Jane Q, husband and wife, as joint tenants. Joint tenancy in marriage is otherwise referred to as "Tenancy-By-The-Entirety".

- TENANTS IN COMMON: In the case of Tenancy In Common, the co-owners own a shared interest in the property, but unlike joint tenancy, the interest or shares need not be quantitatively equal or equal with respect to duration. With Tenants In Common, There is no right of survivorship; the interest of each tenant will vest in their heirs or devisee upon their decease. Vesting for Tenants In Common might appear as: John Q, a single man, as to an undivided 3/4^{ths} interest, and Tom Jones, a single man, as to an undivided 1/4th interest, as tenants in common.

- TRUST: In California, title to real property may be held in trust; in such case, the Trust entity holds legal and equitable title to the property (rather the individual or co-owners). The trustee holds title for the benefit of the trustor (beneficiary) who retains all of the management rights and responsibilities of the estate.

V.I.V.A.: Verified Income, Verified Assets (typically an easier qualification and better rate than a S.I.V.A., S.I.S.A. or N.I.V.A.

Why? Because a fully documented and verified situation is lower risk than a stated one - or partially stated one).

V. O. D.: Verification Of Deposit (by lender).

V. O. E.: Verification Of Employment (by lender).

V. O. M.: Verification Of Mortgage (by lender).

V. O. R.: Verification Of Rent (by lender).

WARRANTABLE [Condos]: A condominium project that is conformable to "Fannie" and "Freddie" guidelines to be sold to either on the "secondary market" - of which, Freddie and Fannie are the largest investors. (Conversely, non-warrantable condos are not eligible to be sold to Fannie Mae and Freddie Mac). Most lenders therefore will not lend on non-warrantable condos; as a result, non-warrantable condos are viewed as risky, as reflected and/or compensated for in higher down payment and interested rates of such loans.

WARRANTY: A legal, binding, promise, given at the time of a sale, whereby the seller gives the buyer certain assurances as to the condition of the property being sold. Warranties for real property have become less prevalent with the increase of title insurance. A general warranty deed operates to guarantee that the grantor (seller) holds clear title to a piece of real estate and has a right to sell it. The guarantee is not limited to the time the grantor owned the property, but extends back to the property's origins. Important features of a general warranty are:

- The grantor states that they are in deed the owner of the property and have the right to sell it.

- The grantor assures there are no hidden liens, debts or other encumbrances on the property, besides that which appears in the public records.

- The grantor guarantees the grantee (new owner) compensation for any losses incurred from error, omissions or other discrepancies with title.

WEIGHTED AVERAGE: Averaging by taking into account the proportional relevance of each of various components, rather than treating them equally.

WET STATE vs. DRY STATE: A "wet" state is a state (within the U.S.A.) whose laws dictate that once doc's are drawn for a borrower's signature (whether signed or not), the lender is bound to fund the loan and cannot renege without facing a penalty. As such, lenders in wet states typically require that all conditions (PTD & PTF) be met prior to doc's being drawn. Conversely, a "dry" state is one where the lender has the option to renege on funding after the loan documents have been drawn without suffering a penalty.

WHOLESALE: (A Broker), also called indirect lending. Brokers, working with multiple direct lenders, tend to have a broader range of products and greater pricing flexibility than direct lenders (who only work within their portfolio). NOTE: As a rule, in a finance or refinance transaction with brokers, a client's credit report is pulled twice: once by the broker and again by the direct lender taking the loan.

Y.S.P.: Yield Spread Premium (also referred to as "yield spread", "rebate" or "back-end" point(s). In addition to the origination/front-end points, the YSP contributes to the commission on the loan.

SECTION 2

BY THE NUMBERS

Following are numeric codes that relate to particular aspects of conventional residential mortgage lending:

3-DAY RIGHT OF RECISION: There is a Federal 3-day right-of-rescission period (excluding Sundays and holidays) allowing the borrower time to study and accept or reject the loan proposal. There is no right of rescission period for residential mortgage purchases. The ink is dried upon signing.

§32/"HOEPA": (the Home Ownership & Equity Protection Act) is more commonly referred to as *"Section 32"* or the "high-cost" limit rule. This cost-controlling regulation dictates that the total costs (i.e. fees + points) of a first-position lien/loan - before or at closing - cannot exceed whichever is the larger of $499.00 (as of 2004) or 8% of the total loan amount, and/or that the APR cannot exceed - by more than 10 percentage points - the rates on Treasury securities of comparable maturity.

- In conventional mortgage lending, the standard approach is to limit the costs of a loan <= $250,000.00 to 6% of the total loan amount, and 7.5% on loans =>$250,000.00. To simplify matters, lenders multiply the total loan amount by 5.99% to ascertain the maximum cost figure, so as to stay safely within the bounds of the regulation. (The costs of a loan include escrow, title, processing, administrative, wire, doc' drawing, notary fees, front and back-end points, discount/buy-down, buy-up points, &c).

DELINQUENCIES: 0x30, 1x30, 2x30, 3x30 / 0x60, 1x60 2x60 / 1x90, 2x90: The number on the left of the slash mark represents the number of times that a borrower has made a late payment within the expressed time period, and the number on the right of the slash mark represents the delinquency period in terms or blocks of days, representing months: 30 = 1 month [late], 60 = 2 months [late], 90 = 3 months [late], 120 = 4 months [late].

In other words, 0x30 means that the borrower has had zero or no thirty-day late payments within a given time period (usu. 12 months for sub-prime and ALT-A lenders, and may be 24 months or longer with prime lenders). 1x60 means that a borrower was sixty days or two months late on a payment one time within the time period. 2x90 would mean that the borrower has been 90 days or three months late two times within the given time period.

422 - Follow-up appraisal.

433 (or 413) - referred to as 'Permanent Foundation Certification', regarding mobile/manufactured houses. It is used to signify, classify or certify the property as "real" rather than "personal" property (again, when a structure has wheels and/or an axel and/or a towing device attached, it is "mobile" and therefore, categorically "personal" property. "Real" property is "immobile". Classification 433 has different letter designations that represent different things:

- A 433a is the form that is recorded in the county where the property is located; however, a 433a can exist and yet not be recorded.

- A 433b is merely an informational certificate to clarify assessments and ownership, etc.

- A 433c is the local building inspector's certificate that shows habitability.

  (Although "433" is the common code related to Permanent Foundation Certification, different authorities or agencies may use different codes, specific to their system but that speak to the same thing).

1003 - The legal "Uniform Residential Loan Application".

1004 - The Appraisal.

1008 - The loan "Transmittal Summary".

1031 Exchange - As per IRC (Internal Revenue Code) §1.1031, a properly structured 1031-exchange allows an investor to sell a property, to reinvest the proceeds in a new property and to defer all capital gains taxes. IRC §1031 (a)(1) states: *"No gain or loss shall be recognized on the exchange of property held for productive use in a trade or business or for investment, if such property is exchanged solely for property of like-kind which is to be held either for productive use in a trade or business or for investment."* Exchanges protect investors from capital gains taxes and can facilitate significant portfolio growth, change, diversification, consolidation and increased return on investment(s). A real property owner can sell his property and reinvest the proceeds in ownership of "Like-Kind" property - *held for productive use in a trade or business or for investment purposes* - and defer the capital gains taxes. Both the property sold and the property received must be of "Like-Kind". It is the use of the property that determines its classification.

- Within a strict 45 calendar-day period (admitting no allowance for weekends or legal holidays) the owner/seller of the relinquished property must identify suitable replacement properties. The taxpayer must receive the replacement property within the "exchange period", which ends within the earlier of 180 days after the date on which the taxpayer transfers the property relinquished or the due date for the taxpayer's tax return for the taxable year in which the transfer of the relinquished property occurs. As with the 45-day rule the 180-day rule is very strict and is not extended if the 180th day should happen to fall on a Saturday, Sunday or legal holiday.

- The replacement property must be subject to an equal level or greater level of debt than the relinquished property or the buyer will either have to pay taxes on the amount of the decrease or have to put in additional cash funds to offset the lower level of debt in the replacement property.

- All cash proceeds from the original sale must be reinvested in the replacement property to qualify for tax deferment. Cash proceeds not reinvested are taxable. The proceeds from the sale must go through the hands of a "Qualified Intermediary" for the proceeds to be tax-deferred. If the proceeds from the sale go through the hands of the seller or an agent of theirs, the proceeds will become taxable.

4506 - IRS form 4506 is used to request a copy of a transcript of a borrower's tax form for a given year. When a borrower signs form 4506, it authorizes a lender to obtain a copy of their tax return(s) from the Internal Revenue Service, which is used by the lender to confirm a borrower's "income" (which may or may not have been fraudulently reported). Lenders will compare the numbers from the 4506 with the numbers on the copies of tax documentation in the file as submitted by the borrower to prove the accuracy or inaccuracy of information.

"ZERO-TO-60"

In a perfect-world scenario, a residential mortgage loan can be completed, start-to-finish, within 10 days or less; in a normal-world scenario, 15 to 30 days; in a worse case scenario, 45 days or longer.

SECTION 3

STEPS OF THE LOAN PROCESS

The following order is a guideline and typical sequence of events in the processing of a loan; however, the order may vary and certain steps within the process can be and often are covered simultaneously.

1. App' it: Take a complete loan application "handwritten 1003".

2. Comp' it: Get property comparables; figure the property value and the loan LTV.

3. Price it: Use lender's pricing matrix to determine the interest rate, payment, savings, Cash-out, etc.

4. Pitch it: Explain loan proposal and benefits to client.

5. Credit: If client accepts proposal, acquire their credit report(s) by their permission.

6. Doc' it: If credit qualifies, obtain required documentation from the borrower: disclosures, declaration of insurance, mortgage note or statement, "income" doc's and current statements for accounts to be paid off through the loan.

7. Enter it: Enter data electronically or "type" the 1003.

8. Open it: Open Escrow, order Preliminary Report and Payoff demands.

9. Appraise it: schedule an appraisal with an appraiser and the client.

10. Submit it: (Most sub-prime lenders will accept a 1003, 1008 and credit report for preliminary pricing). Send a hard copy of a full package (1003, 1008, credit report, prelim', appraisal and income doc's) to lender for final approval.

11. Stip' it: Get outstanding stipulations/conditions from the lender. Satisfy all.

12. Sign it: Once all stip's have been met, the loan doc's can be drawn for the borrower's signature.

13. Hold it: 3-day rescission period (excluding Sundays and holidays) allowing the borrower time to accept or reject the loan. (Does not apply to purchases).

14. Fund it: Normally on the fourth day (excluding Sundays and holidays), Escrow funds the loan.

15. Disperse and close it: Typically, on the fifth day (excluding Sundays and holidays), all monies are dispersed, all parties are paid and the loan closes.

SECTION 4

REASONS TO REFI'

1. GET MONEY

2. SAVE MONEY

3. RATE & TERM (to $ave money)

4. DEBT CONSOLIDATION (to $ave money)

5. HOME IMPROVEMENT (to get money - "cash-out")

6. INVESTMENT/WEALTH-BUILDING (to get money - "cash-out")

LOAN PRODUCTS:

1. FIXED (Long Term)

2. A.R.M. (Short Term)

3. COMBINATION ("PIGGY-BACK") LOAN

4. STAND-ALONE SECOND

5. I/O (Interest Only)

6. NEG' AM'/Negative Amortization (subprime product)

7. PAYMENT OPTION A.R.M. (subprime product)

8. REVERSE MORTGAGE

9. [H].E.L.O.C. (2nd position lien)

(The first two reasons - getting money or saving money - are the basis of all other reasons for refinancing).

FIXED (LONG-TERM) **LOANS:**
<u>(PROS & CONS)</u>

GENERAL PROS:
Undisturbed interest rate - promotes a sense of stability.
The longer the term, the lower the monthly payment

GENERAL CONS:
Besides effectively paying for the property 2 to 3 times over,
owing to long-term interest, there are no cons.

40/40
Payment schedule amortized over forty years, due in forty-
years, stable rate.

40/30
Payment schedule amortized over forty years, due in thirty
years - with a balloon.

Pro(s)
Lightest payment schedule offered on long-term loan
products.

Con(s)
Takes longer to build equity than shorter terms because a
smaller percentage of the monthly payment goes toward
reducing principle.
Homeowner pays more interest (min. 10 years worth) over
shorter terms if they go full term.

30/30
Payment schedule amortized over thirty years, due in thirty
years.

Pro(s)
Light payment schedule
Stable rate.

Con(s)
N/A

30/15

(*This product is for a second position lien*)
Payment schedule amortized over thirty years, due in fifteen years with a balloon.

Pro(s)
30-year pricing for a lower payment on a 2nd mortgage, which normally has a shorter term with a higher payment.

Con(s)
Balloon payment the 15th year.

20/20

Payment schedule amortized over twenty years, due in twenty years.

Pro(s)
Shorter term with substantial savings on interest over a 30-year term.

Con(s)
Higher payment than a thirty-year term: upwards of $200.00 to $300.00 more per month.

15/15

Payment schedule amortized over fifteen years, due in fifteen years.

Pro(s)
Shorter term, with substantial savings on interest - over a 30-year term.

Con(s)
Higher payment than a thirty-year term: upwards of $400.00 to $500.00 more per month.

(With compressed long terms (i.e. 20/20, 15/15), the savings in interest outweighs the increase in payment)

A.R.M. (or SHORT-TERM) LOAN PRODUCTS.
(PROS & CONS)

- 2/38 = 40 years (2 years fixed, 38 years adjustable)
- 2/28 = 30 years (2 years fixed, 28 years adjustable)
- 3/27 = 30 years (3 years fixed, 27 years adjustable)
- 5/25 = 30 years (5 years fixed, 25 years adjustable)
- 7/23 = 30 years (7 years fixed, 23 years adjustable)
- 10/20 = 30 years (10 yrs. fixed 20 years adjustable)

GENERAL PROS:
Interest rate is up to 75 bps lower than long-term/fixed products resulting in (short-term) savings. Homeowners can use the brief fixed period to improve their payment history/credit profile and position themselves to qualify for a better long-term fixed interest rate in the near future.

GENERAL CONS:
Short-term fixed period
Loan becomes subject to market volatility when adjustable.

INTEREST ONLY

Pro(s)
Lower payment than a fully amortized loan resulting in savings.

Con(s)
Pays interest portion only - does not pay down principal.

NEGATIVE AMORTIZATION

Pro(s)
Minimal payment
Improved cash flow

Con(s)
Loan balance may gradually increase - by the difference between the minimum payment rate and the fully indexed rate payment; create a balloon at the end of the term and absorb equity.

PAYMENT OPTION A.R.M. OPTIONS:

1. Negative Amortization/"deferred interest"/"minimum payment" (see explanation above).
2. Interest Only (see above explanation).
3. 30-year [adjustable] *amortization*. Certain lenders may advertise a "fixed period", but that may only relate to stabilizing the minimum payment for the "fixed period", rather than providing a "fixed *rate*").
4. 15-year [adjustable] *amortization*.

> Pro(s)
> Payment flexibility
> Savings potential
> Particularly good for self-employed or seasonal employment
>
> Con(s)
> All options are A.R.M.'s.
> Neg' Am' payment may increase mortgage balance, absorb equity and create a balloon

---

> **REVERSE MORTGAGE**
>
> Pro(s)
> Mortgage pays homeowner rather than homeowner paying mortgage
> Targeted for elderly persons (min. age 62)
>
> Con(s)
> Loan must be repaid (advances plus interest) if homeowner vacates the property (but not being deceased) for twelve consecutive months.

> **H.E.L.O.C.**
>
> Pro(s)
> Smaller (second) loan amount - by comparison to first position lien.
> Traditionally lower interest rates and costs than a full refinance.
> Usually only interest payment required
>
> Con(s)
> Hard to qualify for in sub-prime

<u>TIME LIMITATIONS</u>

APPRAISAL: Stale after 3 to 6 months (depending on the lender's criteria). Within the period that the appraisal is viable, the borrower can ask the appraiser to change the name of the lender on the report to the name of another lender for a fee. A "recert'" (recertification of the appraisal) may be necessary and may be gotten from the appraiser (again, for a fee) to keep the appraisal valid within the period specified by the lender).

CREDIT REPORT: Stale after 45 - 60 days.

CREDIT REPORT SCORE REDUCTION: Limited to mortgage and auto: theoretically, any number of inquiries made within a 14-day period is treated as a single inquiry and purportedly does not cause a reduction of the consumer's credit score. Inquiries made outside of mortgage and auto concerns will count as a separate inquiry each time credit is run, which may cause a reduction in the credit score by 1 point per repository, per inquiry - if not more.

"INCOME" DOCUMENTS: Stale after 30 days.

PRELIMINARY/TITLE REPORT: Good for up to 90 days, after which time it may be backdated or updated to reflect the most current status of information. Understanding the time limitations (particularly with the credit report and income doc's) can - and should be - used to instill a sense of urgency in the loan process for the borrower as well as the L.O.

IMPORTANT

RE: REFINANCE:

1. Ask the borrower if they currently have a prepayment penalty.

2. Ask the borrower if their current mortgage is impounded/escrowed, and if they would you like their new mortgage to be impounded/escrowed.

3. Ask the borrower if their current mortgage has P.M.I.

RE: [HOME] PURCHASE MONEY:

1. Ask the buyer if they have money to apply toward a down payment and/or closing costs, and if so, how much.

2. Inquire the buyer about their general credit profile and if they know their credit score.

3. Ask the buyer what would be the highest mortgage payment they can reasonably handle and what their total (and consistent) monthly earnings are.

SECTION 5

PURCHASE MONEY SKETCH

PREQUALIFICATION: Following is a sketch of how the residential home purchase process works. It is important that the L.O. maintain close contact with the real estate agent through each step of the transaction.

After ascertaining the buyer's down-payment limit, credit complexion, and monthly earnings:

1. DETERMINE THE BUYER'S MAX. MORTGAGE PAYMENT:

    Multiply the borrower's monthly earnings by the maximum debt ratio percentage factor allowed by the lender: .50 (50%) for sub-prime, .45 (45%) for ALT-A, and .35 (35%) for prime, and reduce that figure by the borrower's credit-reporting monthly outgo to arrive at their maximum monthly mortgage payment. (Be sure to account for Taxes and Insurance if payment is to be impounded). With the maximum mortgage payment established, the total loan amount can be determined (see calculation below) so that the client will know what their property value limit is when they go house-hunting.

2. DETERMINE THE INTEREST RATE:

    With knowledge of the purchaser's credit profile/score and LTV, ascertain the interest rate from the lenders' pricing matrix or A. E. (Account Executive) and factor that into the mortgage calculation to firm or refine pricing and see if it alters any aspect(s) of the program initially discussed with the buyer.

3. DETERMINE DOWN PAYMENT AND CLOSING COSTS:

Determine the down payment required and the non-recurring closing costs, and the borrower's ability to satisfy either or both (this will influence the type of program offered, i.e., a "straight" or "combo" loan. This can also determine whether a "seller private-party carry-back" can be useful and how necessary a "seller contribution" might be). Note: applicable closing costs (recurring: Insurance, Interest and Taxes, and non-recurring: all other fees and points) are to be paid "outside of closing" by the buyer.

4. PRE-APPROVAL LETTER AND DISCLOSURES:

A pre-qualification letter should be provided in the potential buyer's name(s), featuring the salient points of qualification, such as the maximum loan amount and Loan To Value. The pre-qualification letter should be sent to the real estate agent or seller with the disclosure forms, and a copy of the pre-qualification letter should be sent to the buyer.

5. MISCELLANY:

- Purchaser's credit must be run to confirm eligibility for loan program.

- Loan to be structured and supported by required documentation and satisfaction of conditions to confirm program soundness.

- Purchases do not include debt consolidation or "cash-out" as such (however cash may be creatively routed to the borrower from the seller via the seller contribution procedure).

6. PROPERTY:

Urge the client to (readily) find and settle on a property (within their total loan amount/mortgage payment range).

7. PURCHASE CONTRACT:

Seller and Buyer creates a purchase agreement outlining terms and conditions.

8. OPEN ESCROW:

The seller or agent representing the seller opens escrow and orders the preliminary report.

9. APPRAISAL/PROPERTY INSPECTION:

Appraisal and property (termite) inspection(s) are done to validate property value and loan legitimacy (seller and purchaser decides who pays for either).

10. Loan officer (processor) gathers and coordinates necessary documents for loan submission and final approval.

11. After stip's are satisfied, the loan can be doc'd, signed, funded and closed (with no 3-day right of recision).

SECTION 6

MORTGAGE CALCULATOR BASICS

The following instructions are generic in nature and as a rule work for most mortgage calculators, as most operate by the same principle.

Make sure the calculator is set in the proper mode to compute mortgage payments based on a 12 (month) pay-period schedule (manufacturer's manual or tech' support should provide instructions on how to do so).

By entering the numeric value of four of the five function keys, the value or answer of the fifth function key is automatically computed.

CALCULATING THE MORTGAGE PAYMENT:

Enter the numeric value (in any sequence) of each function key except the payment (PMT) KEY which is to be entered last of all to calculate the monthly payment.

N = Number of years/amortization (expressed in years or months, depending on the calculator's design)
I/YR or INT. = Interest Rate
PV or LA = Present Value / Loan Amount (i.e. the total loan amount)
FV = Future Value (optional key – value: usually 0)
PMT = PayMentT (for monthly mortgage payment)

Any one of the function values may be changed individually (as an aspect of the calculation may change, e.g. modified loan amount, interest rate or term of years) without it disturbing the other set values. This allows for quick and easy recalculation of a loan.

Enter the numeric value for each of the function keys except for the interest rate (INT. / I/YR) key, which is to be entered last of all to calculate the interest rate. The following order works on most mortgage calculators. Enter the:

1. Number of years/amortization (expressed in years or months)

2. Loan Amount or Present Value or the Loan Amount (as a positive value)

3. PayMenT as a negative value: (enter the payment value and depress the +/- key, then press the PMT key)

4. Future Value (numeric value, typically 0)

5. I/YR or INT. key (to get the Interest Rate)

BASIC MORTGAGE CALCULATIONS

AVERAGING RATES: When a borrower has more than one loan with differing interest rates, add the rates together and divide them by the number of loans they represent. Example:

<table>
<tr><td>

1st 6.0% +
2nd 11.5%
÷   2
8.75%

</td><td>

1st 5.5% +
2nd 9.0% +
3rd 14.0% +
÷   3
9.50%

</td></tr>
</table>

BIWEEKLY PAYMENT CALCULATION: The face mortgage payment divided by 2 and that, multiplied by 26. (The difference between 12 [annual] and 26 [biweekly] payments amounts to an extra payment in a year, which has the effect of shortening the loan term by as many as five years. Example:

$ 1,200.00 (x 12 = $14,400 in a year)
÷   2
$ 600.00
X   26
$15,600.00 ($15,600 – $14,400 = $1,200)

BLENDING RATES: 80/20 Combo: Multiply the first rate by 80. Multiply the second rate by 20. Add the two products together and then divide the sum by 100. (With other combinations, multiply the rates by the ratios expressed; e.g. 80/10, 70/20, 70/15).

1st 5.5%	2nd 9.0 %	440	620
X 80	X 20	+ 180	÷ 100
440	180	620	6.20

COST CALCULATION: Multiply the total loan amount by the cost factor in percentage form and add that figure to the previous total loan amount for the new loan amount. Example:

$250,000.00 (original total loan amount)
X   2.5% (cost factor)
$ 6,250.00 (cost figure)

$250,000.00
+ $6,250.00
$256,250.00 (new total loan amount)

CREDIT CARD ("REVOLVING DEBT") PAYMENT CALCULATION: When the payment is not indicated, it is assumed that the minimum percentage paid is between 2%-4% (presently, at least). Multiply the opening balance of the loan by 2% to 3% to deduce the possible minimum monthly payment on the loan. Example:

$1,200.00
X   0.025
$ 30.00

DEBT TO INCOME RATIO: Divide the monthly outgo by the monthly in-come (usually 40% - 55% maximum, depending on the lender's criteria). Example:

$1,200.00 (outgo)
÷$2,400.00 (in-come)
50% (DTI)

DISCOUNT/BUY-DOWN POINTS: (the ratio varies from
lender to lender, however, on average) 1 discount point will
reduce the interest rate by up to ½ of a point. Many if not most
lenders allow a maximum of 2 discount/buy-down points. In
some cases, after the first discount point, additional discount
points may be affected by "compression" which means that the
rate reduction lessens with each additional buy-down point.
(**NOTE:** Commission is not paid on buy-down monies - that goes
to compensate the lender for reducing the rate). Example:

6.5 % (starting rate)	6.0% (adjusted rate)
1st buy-down point	2nd discount point
(- .50 "ratio")	(- .375 "compression")
6.0%	5.63%

HAZARD INSURANCE CALCULATION: Multiply the
beginning or opening balance of the mortgage loan by the
(present) industry-standard factor of 0.0035 to arrive at the
annual hazard insurance amount, and divide that number by 12
to arrive at the monthly hazard insurance amount. Example:

$200,000.00	$ 200,000.00
X 0.0035	X .35 %
$ 700.00	$ 700.00
÷ 12	÷ 12
$58.33	$58.33

INTEREST ONLY (monthly) **PAYMENT CALCULATION:**
The loan amount under consideration multiplied by the
applicable interest rate, and that divided by 12. (The calculation
may be expressed in decimal or percentage form on a calculator).
Example:

$100,000.00
X   .055
(or 5.5%)
$ 5,500.00
÷   12
$ 458.33

LOAN TO VALUE: Divide the total loan amount by the property Value (the lower the LTV, the lower the risk and thus the better the interest rate – and vice-versa). Example:

$ 200,000.00 (Loan Amount)
÷$250,000.00 (Property Value)
80%

PREPAYENT PENALTY CALCULATION: The product of 5 to 6 times the monthly interest portion of the opening loan amount, or: multiply the opening loan amount by 2% - 3%, or, to be more exact, multiply the opening loan balance by 80% and multiply that factor by the interest rate of the loan and divide that figure by 2 to arrive the prepayment penalty amount.

$250K P.V.	$250,000.00	$250,000.00
6.5% I. R.	X 2.5%	X 80%
360 mo. Term	$ 6,250.00	$200,000.00
$1,580.17 Pmt		X 6.5% I.R.
X 80% Int.		$13,000.00
$1,264.14 X 5		÷ 2
$ 6,320.70		$6,500.00

PREPAYMENT PENALTY BUY-OUT RATIO: Buying out the prepayment penalty is possible but may cost the borrower in excess of a 1.0% increase in the interest rate to completely buy out the P.P.P. or as much as a .50% increase in the interest rate for each individual year bought out.

PROPERTY TAX CALCULATION: (Other than looking on the comp's for the annual property taxes), multiply the beginning or opening balance of the loan amount by the industry-standard factor (presently .0125%) to arrive at the annual tax amount and divide that number by 12 to arrive at the monthly amount. Example:

```
        $300,000.00
        X       .0125
        (or    1.25%)
        $    3,750.00
        ÷             12
        $       312.50
```

SECTION 7

INTERPRETING CREDIT

- TRADE INFORMATION: Marks and sequence differ from reporting agency to reporting agency, but in some form or fashion, credit reports feature the following information relative to credit activity:

- Creditor Name and Account Number.

- Date Reported and "DLA": Date of Last Activity.

- Date Opened: The date the account was originally started.

- High Credit/Credit Limit: The opening balance of the loan or highest amount allowed or utilized.

- Balance Owing or Amount Past Due: Reflects only the remaining principle balance due (not accounting for or reflecting the interest paid on a loan (even I/O and Neg. Am. loans).

- Terms: The monthly payment amount.

- Account Type: MTG = Mortgage. INST = Installment debt (e.g. auto, student loan, mechanics lien, and even second mtgs.). REV = Revolving (i.e. credit card) debt.

- Current Status: CURR = Current payment(s) history. SLOW = Slow payment(s).

- ECOA (Equal Credit Opportunity Act): Shows the manner in which the loan was acquired: I – Individually, J = Jointly, U = Unknown or Undetermined).

- "Whose" = Who is responsible for the debt: B = Borrower. O = Other.

- # Mo./Mos. Rev.: The number of months an account has been active or reporting or 'revolving'.

- Times past Due: Indicates how many times a payment has been as late as 30-59, 60-89, 90-119 and even 120 days.

- STS: STATUS of an account. 5 = Paid collection account. 6 = N.O.D. 7 = Bankruptcy (chp. 7). 8 = Foreclosure. 9 = Collection or charge-off account.

- Loan Term: The number of years/months the loan is scheduled to be paid off.

- Payment or Late Grid: Shows the payment history in numeric code: An X or dash mark (-) signifies not reported and/or late, but not as many as 30 days late. 1 (or "C") signifies timely or current payments.   2 signifies 30 days late. 3 signifies 60 days late. 4 signifies 90 days late. 5 signifies 120 days late. The first number on the extreme left of the grid represents the current month. Counting twelve characters backward from that point encompasses a year.

- Public Record: Shows information on bankruptcies, liens and judgments against the borrower.

- Inquiries: Shows how many inquiries have been made on the borrower's credit and over what period of time.

CREDIT RISK FACTORS - BY PERCENTAGE

35% - PAYMENT HISTORY:

How timely a consumer pays their debts (derogatory activity is viewed over the last 3 years).

30% - DEBT LOAD:

Meaning how much debt is owed at the end of a month - credit card debt being the most problematic. (Note: the higher the percentage of available revolving credit used, the higher the risk factor). Also, closure of revolving/credit card accounts does not necessarily increase one's score, and in fact may temporarily lower the score, as it momentarily raises the overall percentage of credit used. An account balance exceeding 50% of the high credit limit negatively affects credit and works to suppress the credit score; therefore, keeping the credit card balances below 50% of the high credit limit is best as it works to raise the credit score. An increase in a credit card limit may also result in lowering the usage limit to at or below 50%.

15% - CREDIT HISTORY:

30 years of credit history is the marker for "long" credit history. However 3 to 5 years credit history is adequate for a credit rating agency or a lender to make a determination of one's "credit worthiness".

Formula for calculating revolving credit history: The number of credit cards divided by the length of credit history. For example, a consumer owning 2 credit cards for five years has a credit history of 2.5 years. Adding 3 new credit cards in a short period of time in this case would substantially reduce the appearance of the credit history according to the formula.

The 2 old credit cards plus the 3 new credit cards, equaling 5 credit cards - in 5 years works out to 5 ÷ 5 or a credit history of 1 year.

10% - TYPE OF ACCOUNT ACTIVITY:

If there is a revolving account with no activity within the last six months, that account will not be used in determining the credit score unless money is owed on the account, especially when the balance exceeds 50% of the high credit limit.

10% - NEW INQUIRIES: An "inquiry" is when credit is run.

See Credit/Fico score definition above.

SECTION 8

PROPERTY AND APPRAISAL

"Appraisers are not inspectors; in other words, we do not look for or report what we do not obviously detect" – certified residential property appraiser.

RE: APPEARANCE

"An appraisal paints a picture", an appraiser once said, and: "lenders view appraisal photos in the same way that anyone would"; in other words, the better kept the property, the better impression it makes with the lender. Conversely, unkempt property makes a bad impression with the lender, whose appraisal review committee validates or invalidates appraised values based on the appearance of things. Therefore, "Curb appeal" (the way the property looks from the outside) and "Home Pride" (the way the property looks on the inside) is a matter of practical importance. Also, an appraiser once advised that, if and when possible, there should be as few individuals as possible in or on the property at the time the appraisal is conducted, as it "looks better".

RE: UPGRADES

Home improvement is always good as it adds value to property; however, there is such a thing as over improvement that may not yield the level of property appreciation that might be expected.

RULE: The three largest homes in the immediate vicinity limit(s) the value of the subject property, regardless of the upgrades. For example: A residential property that has been upgraded from a 3/2 to a 6/4 (bed/bath), as compared to the three largest homes in the area that only have the 3/2 combination, will receive minimal value upgrade consideration, owing to the upgrade "rule".

Another example would be a house with a pool, as compared to the three largest houses in the same area not having a pool. The property with a pool would receive only minimal value upgrade consideration, owing to the upgrade rule. (There are also occasions when a residential property with a pool that becomes too costly for the homeowner to keep up, and out of liability concerns, has been filled with dirt, to downplay it).

STRUCTURAL vs. COSMETIC UPGRADES:

Structural upgrades, such as a new roof ("composition" roof - good for up to 20 years; "concrete" roof good for up 100 years), a room addition, pool addition or concrete pavement, commands optimum appraisal appreciation, whereas cosmetic upgrades, such as an upgraded kitchen or bathroom, new windows, carpeting, tile, paint, electrical upgrades, etc. may enhance market appeal and possibly command a higher market value, but does not result in property appraisal appreciation like structural upgrades do. Other valuable upgrades include landscaping, such as adding shrubbery and palm trees; flowers, brickwork, fencing and electrical enhancements.

"PERMITTED" vs. "NON-PERMITTED":

It is very important that structural additions be "permitted" by the governing municipality (the city or other, as applicable) in order to be recognized by the lender. Non-permitted additions are suspected of being out of compliance with safety codes and are therefore frowned upon by lenders. If a property was purchased with un-permitted additions, but the appraiser can attest (in the appraisal report) that the additions were performed, made or done in a "professional manner" or "workmanlike fashion" (such verbiage as the lenders require), the lender may accept or ignore the additions and proceed with the loan; otherwise, the property owner would have to go through the time and expense of getting the additions permitted before the lender considers the property acceptable.

RE: LOT SIZE

The average range of the cost of land is .50 - $2.00 per square foot, depending on the area. The lot size of a property does not begin to appreciably impact the value until one property's lot size differs from neighboring properties by 10,000 or so square feet (making a difference of some $5,000.00 -$20,000.00 in the appraised value of the property).

RE: LOCATION AND PROXIMITY

According to one appraiser, very important is a property's location, appearance and proximity to other structures; in other words, the environment of the neighborhood/area. For example, properties near a cemetery, a dump cite or a freeway, or where loiterers are present, may compromise the value of the subject property; whereas properties in well kept neighborhoods, near businesses parks and professional areas tend to hold better value and are granted as much.

RE: VARIANCE

Appraisers can work with a variance factor up to 15% higher than the figures of comparable properties in determining the value of a subject property. Lenders may exercise a plus-or-minus 4% variance factor at their discretion.

RE: ADJUSTMENTS

Adjustments featured in an appraisal report are notations of accoutrements outside the base characteristics of the home like square footage, bed/bath count and year built. Such "adjustments" are used to bolster property value and justify the same. Property values excluding adjustments are considered more solid figures than figures including adjustments and as such, are considered more reliable for comp' purposes.

RE: "442"

If the 1004 (i.e. the initial appraisal) is considered incomplete for any reason, a secondary appraisal, called a "442" may be required by the lender to confirm, reaffirm or disaffirm property value. (Also, it is a good idea to ask the appraiser to include a flood zone certification and a plat map).

RE: THE O.R.E.A.
(The Office of Real Estate Appraisers)

Title XI of the Federal Financial Institutions Reform, Recovery and Enforcement Act of 1989 adopted by congress, mandated states to license and certify real estate appraisers who appraise property for federally related transactions. In response to which, the Real Estate Appraisers Licensing and Certification law was enacted by the California Legislature in 1990 (AB 527, Chapter 491 of 1990).

The O.R.E.A. was established within the Business, Transportation and Housing Agency, and charged with developing and implementing a real estate appraiser licensing and certification program compliant with the federal mandate.

It is The Office of Real Estate Appraisers that governs the protocol of the appraisal process. However, what the OREA allows, a lender may disallow and it is the decision of the lender that ultimately prevails; therefore appraisers bear in mind the limits that lenders set.

<u>MINIATURE SAMPLE PRICING & BENEFITS SHEET</u>

PRICING   BENEFITS

Borrower: ___________________Lender:____________________

Program Type: ____________Monthly Savings: $____________

Credit Score:______________Save next month's mrtg. payment

Derog's:_____________Cash Out amount: $________________

Credit Grade:______ Debt Consolidation: $________$________
                                                  (Monthly) / (Total)
Doc' Type:________________Term/Years:________________

Occupancy Type:__________P&I: $________ / PI/TI: $ _________

L.T.V.: ____% D.R.:____% P.I.T./P.I.I. $______I/O$ ______

Total Loan Amount: $___________Interest Rate:__________%

Date:________________________

Note(s):____

<u>Costs</u>

Mtg. balance(s): $___________Standard Fees:$_____________

Prepayment Penalty: $________Impound reserves: $_________

Cash out: $____________Odd Days Interest: $____________

Debt Consolidation: $________Points________% / $_________

Other (liens, BKs): $______Buy-downs______% / $________

Total Loan amount: $____________________

SAMPLE "INCOME" WORKSHEET

SALARY

Typical "wage" earners' documentation: YTD pay stubs and prior year's W-2.

$_____per pay period X____(pay prds per year*) = $________yr.

(a) $_______________per year ÷ 12 = $_______________per month

(b) $__________Y-T-D ÷_________months = $________per mo.

(c) $________past year ÷_________months = $________per mo.

*If pay stub reflects 86.67 hrs. (on the 15th and end of the month) multiply by 24
*If pay stub reflects 80 hours, multiply by 26
*If pay stub reflects 40 hours, multiply by 52

(NOTE: Figures (b) and (c) help analyze trends. Use only the base pay (salary) when analyzing the pay stub. If YTD earnings include commission, bonus or overtime, and such earnings are being factored for qualifying, it must be calculated based on a 2-year average).

HOURLY

_________hours at \$_________per hour = \$_________per week

\$_________per week X 52 weeks = \$_________per year

(a) \$_________per year ÷ 12 months = \$_________per month

(b) \$_________Y-T-D ÷_________months = \$_________per month

(c) \$_________past year ÷_________months = \$_________per month

(NOTE: Figures (b) and (c) help analyze trends. Use only the base pay (salary) when analyzing the pay stub. If YTD earnings reflect commission, bonus or overtime, and such earnings are being factored for qualifying, it must be calculated based on a 2-year average).

COMMISSION, BONUS AND OVERTIME

\$_________YTD ÷ \$_________past year_________(list year) +

\$_____prior year_____(list year) = \$_____(2 yrs + YTD avg.)

\$_____(2 yrs + YTD avg.) ÷_____total months = \$____per mo.

(NOTE: When considering commissions, bonuses and overtime earnings, a minimal 2-year average is needed, and the "income" should be expected to continue. Patterns of increasing and decreasing "income" ought to also be taken into account over the documented period under consideration).

<h1 style="text-align:center">SAMPLE PROCESSOR'S CHECKLIST</h1>

Loan Officer:____

Borrower:____

Lender:____

Loan Amount: $_______________

Loan Program: Fixed:______________ / A.R.M.____________ / Other:___________

Full Doc':__________ / Stated:________ / Other:__________________

LTV:__________%   CLTV:____________%

Points:____________ / Rebates:____________ / Discount(s):__________

Impounds?______________

Interest Rate:______________%

Processor's Comments:____

____

____

____

____

____

____

____

Title opened with:_____________________________ Date:________________

File sent to:_________________________________ Date:________________

<u>SAMPLE</u> STACKING ORDER AND DOC' CHECKLIST

Submission Sheet

1003/Completed

G.F.E.

1008/Trans. Sum.

Credit Report

Title Report

Payoff Demand

Income Doc's:
(Y-T-D pay stubs, W-2's, or bank
statements or tax returns, Current
mortgage statement, Declaration
of Insurance)

Appraisal

Disclosures

HUD 1

Conversation Log

SCRIPT FRAMEWORK TEMPLATES

SALUTATION/INTRODUCTION:

1. Hello, (or Good morning/afternoon/evening), I'm calling for [first name]. Addressing a client on a first-name basis, though less professional, is a less intimidating.

2. Hello, (or Good morning/afternoon/evening), I'm calling for Mr./Mrs. [last name]. Addressing a client on a last-name basis, though less comfortable is more professional.

The situation and sensitivity ought to dictate.

BASIC SCRIPT IDEAS

Cold-call pitch:

Hi [*person's name*], I am [*your name*] with [*name of institution*] and we are calling homeowners in your area today, offering a free analysis of how new mortgage programs could benefit you by lowering your overall monthly outgo, or putting cash in your pocket for any reason. Have you given thought refinancing recently? If you don't mind my asking: If there was anything about your current mortgage that you could change what would it be? (Listen for 'payment', 'interest rate', 'term' or a need for cash, and proceed to iterate the offer of the analysis - to show how they may accomplish their objective - free of charge).

Special/seasonal greeting pitch:

Hi [*name of person*], my name is [*your name*] with [*name of institution*] and we're calling homeowners in the area now that the expense of (the holiday(s), summer months, graduation, etc.) is behind us to see if you're looking to consolidate debt to lower your monthly outgo or get cash-in-hand for any reason. Would either option be of interest to you at this time?

Warm Lead-sheet pitch:

Hello [*first or last name of person*], I am [*your name*] with [*name of institution*], and I am calling concerning the loan that you took out with [*lender indicated on lead sheet, if provided*] on/in [*date/year indicated*], and my information reflects that the loan is [*an adjustable or a fixed*] at an interest rate of [*if provided*] is that still the case with your loan?

May I ask you [*person's name*]: are you looking to improve your interest rate, lower your monthly outgo or get cash-in-hand for any reason? If "No", thank the homeowner and politely end the call, but if "Yes", proceed with: That sounds good. I can help you. What I would like to do is provide you a free analysis of what we can do together to get that accomplished. I already have much of the information that we require from the data sheet that I have; there are just few more bits of information I will need to gather that will help me complete the analysis for you. (Proceed to gather info. on employment, "income", additional mortgage facts, co-borrower, Social Security Number, etc.)

NOTE: Despite the fact that we always want to sound our best, there is no such thing as a perfect sales pitch because variables differ from encounter to encounter. It is not so much the pitch or polish that makes or breaks an opportunity but the client's need - or the lack thereof - which is what the L.O. should be listening for during the verbal exchange. Pitches are simply guideposts; knowledge is the path, and a client with a need will offer the path of least resistance, and this is where number-crunching becomes valuable: the more calls that are made, the greater the odds of finding a consumer with a need and being able to meet that need according to knowledge. If a need cannot be discovered, then there is little or nothing upon which to build rapport and the endeavor becomes something of a forced-fit, which leaves both parties uncomfortable. But hopefully the L.O. will have had opportunity to explain the value of the services or at least to have made a positive impact on the homeowner so that if and when they do consider refinancing, they'll remember that Loan Officer who made a good impression.

BONUS:

CAR SALES BRASS TACKS

THE 10 STEPS TO A CAR SALE

1. Meet and Greet
2. Establish Rapport
3. Qualify
4. Vehicle Walk Around
5. Test Drive
6. Service Walk & Dealership Tour
7. Offer refreshments
8. Ask for the Sale
9. Offer Write-up & Negotiation
10. Vehicle Delivery

INTRODUCTION AND FACT-FINDING

After a proper and professional introduction and welcome, and learning the client's first and last name and asking if they may be addressed on a first name basis, the salesman should ask:

1) **Are you interested in a car, truck or van**?

2) **New or pre-owned**? (salesman should learn the comparative distinctions between the new and used vehicles; e.g., price: hundreds to thousands of dollars difference, [extended] warranty coverage differences, inspection certification, e.g. "150-point inspection", features and benefits).

3) **Automatic or manual**?

4) **Light or dark color**?

5) **Who is the vehicle is for** (do not assume).

6) What line of work are you in? (to break the ice and coordinate with a particular vehicle).

7) **Are you looking to buy today**?

8) My job is to find you the right vehicle, because if we have the right price but the wrong vehicle, we don't have a deal, do we?

9) **What is your monthly vehicle budget?** If I can make that happen, can we make a deal today? (Note: Roughly, every $10K of car price = $200.00/mo. in car payment. Every 15K in car price = $300.00/mo. in car payment).

10) If it fits in your budget, it'll fit in your garage, right?

11) If I'm able to take $500.00 (or incrementally more) off the window sticker price, would it be worth an hour of your time?

12) **If I could, would you**? (in response to whatever proposal they make). Or: What price of payment would work for you? If I can do that, can we make a deal today? My job is to get you the right price, because if we have the right vehicle but the wrong price, that's a deal-breaker isn't it? And/or: we've never sold a car at a bad price.

13) In the event of rejection of an offer or on a "backstop", ask: We weren't able to meet your needs? What didn't work for you? Or: Was it the man, the money or the machine?

14) During a test-drive, ask: Is there any reason outside of cost, that you wouldn't purchase this vehicle today?

15) When the customer says: "Oh, I'm just lookin'", the salesman might reply to the effect: "no problem; no pressure. I know the lot and inventory well and can help make your search more efficient, so I'll be around to answer any questions you might have." Stand down and let them lead, noting their leanings and offer suggestions when and as appropriate.

CALCULATIONS

TO CALCULATE OR APPROXIMATE THE DOWN PAYMENT:

Multiply the first two numbers of the vehicle price by 3 and add 2 zeros.

TO CALCULATE OR APPROXIMATE THE MONTHLY PAYMENT:

Drop a zero from the approximated down payment.

WHEN A CUSTOMER PROPOSES A MONTHLY PAYMENT:

Multiply the proposed monthly payment by the number of months in the term to arrive at the total cost they would pay for the car to compare with the actual cost of the vehicle, including approx. 12% T&L, to see how realistic or unrealistic their proposal may be.

GLOSSARY

ABS: Anti-lock Braking System

ACV: Actual Cash Value

AWD: All Wheel Drive

BACK-END (money): Gap Insurance, extended warranties and other such "up-sell" items; the lion's share of the commission from which is paid to the finance agent, with some $20.00 - $30.00 in commission, on average, being paid to the car salesman.

BACK OF BOOK: The price or value of a vehicle when it sells below "book" value (as valuated by Kelly Blue Book for example). A vehicle may be bought "below book" by a dealer to allow for wiggle room or profit margin when being priced for sale (in consideration of gross, prep' requirements and so forth).

A vehicle may also be sold "below book" by a private owner either out of ignorance of its fair market value or expedience.

BOOK: The value of a vehicle according to Kelly Blue Book and other such industry-accepted valuation or pricing standards.

FIVE-LINER: The credit application and particularly the first five lines/rows thereof, which capture the essential personal identification aspects of a buyer that the banks require:

Line 1: Last name, first name, middle name, birth date, driver's license, marital status.

Line 2: SSN, ages of dependents.

Line 3(a): Address: street name, number, city, state, zip code, home phone # length of time there.

Line 3(b): Previous address (if current address is <5 years), length of time there, "live in community".

Line 4(a): Occupation, present employer, address, city, state, zip code, phone #, length of time there.

Line 4(b): Previous employment (if at current employer <5 years), address, telephone, length of time stayed.

Line 5: References (relative not living with applicant, name, address, telephone #, relationship).

FLAT: A flat amount (e.g., $500.00 or more [commission/split] added to the price of the vehicle, after it's been sitting an excessive number days (90 days or so) on the floor/lot, as an incentive for the salesman to push and sell it.

FRONT-END: The sales commission (20% on avg.) paid to the car salesperson off of the "gross" or " window" or "sticker" price of a vehicle sold.

FOUR SQUARE: A form or page divided into four equal squares capturing or representing the 4 most immediate (though not all) aspects of a vehicle sale.

Box 1 (upper left): for possible vehicle trade-in value (documenting the vehicle's year, make, model, mileage, cylinders, payoff amount and lien-holder. Buyer is offered an educated-guess figure by the salesman on the value of their vehicle, which should be written down in the box and circled in front of the customer. If the customer objects, the salesman should draw a line through the figure and offer a second and third amount, <u>starting low and moving high</u> incrementally by not more than $100.00 each time in the same fashion. If buyer objects to any or all of the three offers (written, circled and crossed through), the salesman should ask the buyer what they think their vehicle is worth and based on what. Once a figure is satisfactory to the customer, the salesman should write if down, circle it and ask the buyer: "If I could get you that trade-in value, would you take the vehicle today, all things being equal?"

Box 2 (upper right): for the market value or window price of the subject vehicle and add-on equipment if requested by customer. The salesman will also add 10% to the expressed price of the vehicle to cover the non-negotiable T&L. The salesman should write the figure down and circle it in front of the buyer and also have the buyer acknowledge the price of the vehicle and agree with it before moving forward.

Box 3 (lower left): for down payment figuration. The salesman may mention that "the bank may require up to 1/3 of the vehicle value as a down payment to qualify for preferred financing (the salesman should write the figure in the box and circle it in front of the buyer, having them acknowledge and agree to the figure); otherwise, some 12% of the vehicle value is required as a down to cover the non-negotiable tax and license portion of the vehicle" (the salesman should write the figure down in the box and circle it in front of the buyer, having them acknowledge and agree to the figure).

If the customer rejects or cannot provide the 1/3 or 12% figure, the salesman should ask the customer what they can afford and/or write down a minimal figure in the box in front of the buyer and circle it, having the buyer acknowledge and agree to the proposed figure, asking "If I can get the desk to agree to that amount, would you take the vehicle today, all other things being equal?).

Box 4 (lower right): for monthly payment figuration or the amount limited by buyer. Write and circle the rounded figure in the box. <u>Start high and move low</u>, if necessary, not exceeding more than three "hit" figures, and dropping the payment by only $10.00 each time, as each $20.00 dollars represents about $1,000 in profit to the dealership. Write down and circle each figure in the box in front of the customer, drawing a line through each figure rejected by the buyer. Upon reaching a figure the customer agrees to, ask: "If I can get the desk to agree to this monthly payment, would you take the vehicle home today?

GAP INSURANCE: Pays difference between the actual cash value of the vehicle and the current outstanding balance on the vehicle owner's loan or lease, and may or may not pay the vehicle owner's regular insurance deductible. If one's vehicle has been totaled by accident, theft, fire, flood, tornado, hurricane or vandalism, their insurance co. usually pays the actual cash value, which may be less than the vehicle's actual retail value. It is often considerably less than the actual amount the vehicle owner still owes on their loan or the amount due for a lease payoff. The amount between one's insurance deductible and the loss from such a shortfall is the "gap" that one might be left owing, which gap insurance would make up for.

GROSS: Money added to the cost of the car (for profit/commission) after the price of the vehicle was "packed" for safety, smog and such (some $1,500 more packed into the cost of the vehicle to cover such expenses). "Gross" is another term for [the] "window" or "sticker" price of the car; also referred to as "front-end" commission (the salesperson makes on average, 20% commission of the sale price).

HOLD BACK: The percentage of money held back from or determined prior to disclosure of the Manufacturer's Suggested Retail Price (it is undisturbed profit built in to the vehicle for the dealership; e.g. 3% of the MSRP or $800.00 flat, &c).

MARRIAGE: When a Jr. SM turns a customer to a Sr. SM: as long as the Sr. SM is working the customer, the Jr. SM must get back on the point to work for another "up" to compensate the Sr. SM, who would normally get their own "up" by being on point but is out of commission or off the point to work the deal the Jr. SM (salesman) turned to him.

MINI: The minimum commission paid on a new car ($25.00, $50.00, $75.00 and upwards of $100.00 to $150.00 depending on the stores pay plan).

MONEY (LEASE) **FACTOR**: Essentially an auto leasing term that expresses the cost of borrowing money from the bank to finance a car. The money factor determines how much the borrower will pay in finance charges over the life of the lease; the higher the factor, the higher the monthly payment and the more paid in total finance charges (similar but not quite the same as interest on the loan). Though it is an industry-wide thing, the money factor is not a static or industry-standard figure; it varies from leasing co. to leasing company. It is similar to the interest rate paid on a conventional auto loan but is expressed as a difficult-to-understand fraction; notwithstanding, the money factor can be converted into recognizable figure or interest rate or APR (which is what it amounts to) by multiplying the numeric factor by 24 (or 2400 or 2.4 depending on what aspect is being figured). For example, a money factor of .00345 multiplied by 2400 would equal 8.28% or a rounded 9% "interest".

- In order to convert the money factor into an approximate the Annual Percentage Rate, the factor would be multiplied by 2400 when the factor is expressed as a as a decimal, e.g. 0.00345.

- The money factor should be multiplied by 2.4 when it is expressed in percentage form, e.g. 3.45[%] to figure the A.P.R.

- In order to convert the money factor into an interest rate, it would be multiplied by 2,400.

- In order to convert an interest rate into a money factor, it would be divided by 2,400.

- 2400 or 2.4 is used as a "constant" multiplier, regardless of the length of time or money [interest] factor on the lease/loan.

- The money factor, as a rule is not disclosed in most lease contracts, thus, if the buyer does not ask, they will not know.

- The money factor being expressed in decimal form may give the impression that the rate is lower than it really is. It is not until the factor is multiplied by 2400 or 2.4 that the true "interest rate" is divulged.

- The lease payment also has to cover the interest expense associated with the leasing company loaning the buyer the remaining negotiated capitalized cost of the car less any principal repayment over the lease term. <u>In short, the money factor is a number that calculates the interest expense associated with the lease</u>.

MSRP: **M**anufacturer's **S**uggested **R**etail **P**rice. The MSRP (which includes **D**estination and **D**elivery charges) is the price suggested before special options are factored into the bottom line, after which, the price reflected becomes the TSRP, that is, the **T**otal **S**uggested **R**etail **P**rice, as distinct from the MSRP.

NEGATIVE EQUITY: The difference between the [appraised] value of a trade-in vehicle and what the customer owes on it.

For example, if a vehicle appraises for $15,000 but the customer owes $20,000, there is $5,000 in negative equity, also called being "upside down" or "buried", and which the customer is responsible for covering - either out of pocket or by having the negative equity amount added to the price of the vehicle they are buying. The traded in vehicle will be sold for more than the trade-in value given for the vehicle by the receiving dealership that assumes the vehicle with the full expectation of selling it at a profit in the first place, which justifies the trade-in in to begin with.

O.T.D.: The **O**ut **T**he **D**oor price, including the MSRP, options, TSRP, T&L -- in other words, "everything": all costs, fees and such.

PACK(ED): Money added to the selling price of the vehicle to cover or which theoretically accounts for the cost of getting the vehicle road-ready/road-worthy; e.g. smog, certification, safety inspection, replacement tires, cosmetic corrections, glass replacement, etc.)

PDI: **P**re-**D**elivery **I**nspection. The PDI charges are absorbed by the car dealership and by law, are not to be passed on to the buyer. The only fees or charges outside of MSRP that can legally be passed along to the buyer are T & L (Tax and License: some 10% to 12% of the vehicle's selling price), and **DOC'** (document preparation) **FEES**, which are approximately $55.00 for new vehicle and about the same for used.

POUNDER: A multiple of $1,000 in relation to the profit a vehicle (e.g. 2 lbs = $2,000 profit. A 3-pounder is $3,000 profit from the sale of a vehicle).

RESIDUAL: The worth of a vehicle at the end of the lease term - as determined by the bank or lending institution - not the dealership. The typical residual value of a vehicle at the maturity of a lease - all things being equal - is around 40% of the original sales/lease price of the vehicle, give-or-take, on average.

SPOON: A car deal that is more-or-less a done-deal by having been pre-sold or packaged from the desk (i.e. the SM (sales manager), GSM (general sales manager) or GM (general manager) who sit at a desk and "desk" or approve car deals, as opposed to being on point like the salesmen). When the customer comes "up" to the lot to transact the deal, the salesman on point who calls or gets the "up" is to escort the customer to the GSM or GM, as per store/floor protocol, who initiated the deal and who in turn "spoons" or earmarks the deal for the very salesman who took the "up" (in a perfect world, that is).

UNWIND: A vehicle that has to be returned to the car dealership after having been sold/bought in good faith, but for which, the buyer was not able to secure financing (and not able pay cash).